BRINGING HOME THE BACON

AND

CUTTING THE MUSTARD

BRINGING HOME
THE BACON
and
CUTTING THE
MUSTARD

CASTLE BOOKS

This edition published in 2002 by

CASTLE BOOKS ®

A division of Book Sales, Inc.
114 Northfield Avenue
Edison, New Jersey 08837

This edition published by arrangement with and permission of

Complete Editions
London SW13 9RU
United Kingdom

Typeset by David Onyett, Publishing & Production Services,
Cheltenham, United Kingdom

ISBN: 0-7858-1611-9

Printed in the United States of America

INTRODUCTION

———

Ever since the story of Adam tasting the forbidden fruit in the Garden of Eden was first told in the Book of Genesis, food and food-related sayings have been influential ingredients in the development of language.

In the case of English, words and expressions from the kitchen and meal table, the farmyard and the market have been introduced and adapted from other languages since earliest times. From the Romans we acquired references to 'salt' in the sense of 'wages'; 'vintage' as a definition of special quality; and 'larder' as a place to store provisions.

From just across the English Channel, French has supplied numerous expressions and turns of phrase to do with food and drink. Some like *à la carte* and *table d'hôte* have been imported directly into our everyday speech. Others have endured a more tortuous translation: 'bully beef' and 'plonk' both started life in French before their enthusiastic adoption by British servicemen resulted in the forms we use today.

China supplied us with 'cha', the early language of Haiti gave us 'barbecue', Dutch inspired 'cookie', Gaelic (appropriately) gave rise to 'whisky', from Arabic we acquired 'coffee', Portuguese produced 'marmalade' and the language of the Aztecs gave us 'chocolate'. If English cuisine is sometimes accused of being insular and unimaginative, the same cannot be said of the language, which has been nourished and enriched by that of other countries throughout its history.

The 'language of food' reflects something of that history as well; not just in the diversity of sources which came with the expansion of the British Empire and the development of North America, but in the use to which that language has been put. At a basic level, the words for livestock and the meat they produce reveal the social hierarchy that was established in England after the Norman Conquest. We learn something of medieval hospitality and the social order of the Middle Ages from expressions such as 'above the salt' and 'upper crust'.

The important part played in earlier times by the pig is revealed in long-established expressions like 'bringing home the bacon', 'living high off the hog' and 'bacon brains'.

But this is not a sterile process, frozen in time. Expressions like 'Where's the beef?', 'beefcake' and 'couch potato' have been coined and achieved widespread popularity within the last thirty years.

Certain individuals, notably Dame Nellie Melba and the Earl of Sandwich, have guaranteed their place in the history of English through the popularity of Melba toast and the ubiquitous sandwich. Others, like Hiram Codd and Ben Wenberg may have been slightly less fortunate, but the role they played in the evolution of English is described in the pages that follow.

The history of the language also shows how the meanings of some words have changed over time. 'Venison' started out as a general term for food gained in the course of a hunt; only later did it acquire the specific reference it has today. The same is true of 'claret'.

The changing process of cookery itself is also reflected in many things we say and write today. 'Done to a turn' and 'the pot calling the kettle black' hark back to a time when all cooking was done over an open fire, before that was superseded by the use of stoves which gave rise to expressions like 'on the back burner'.

Then there are those quirks and anomalies which give language its spice and variety. In the case of food and drink 'Welsh rarebit', 'Bombay duck' and even the seemingly obvious 'ploughman's lunch' make us pause and smile when we discover the story behind their usage.

From 'off his noodle' to 'nutty as a fruitcake' and from the 'salt of the earth' to 'smart cookie' the English language has a feast of fascinating origins and histories waiting to be enjoyed.

Only a selection can be covered here, but the hope is that *Bringing Home the Bacon and Cutting the Mustard* will provide an appetizing entrée as well as food for thought.

A la carte

This expression, like so many in the language of wining and dining, comes directly from French in which a *carte* was originally a 'card', or a sheet of paper. In a restaurant the *carte* is the bill of fare, the menu on which individual dishes are priced separately. Selecting a meal *à la carte* means choosing dishes from the menu, as opposed to ordering *table d'hôte*, in which case you are served a set meal at a fixed price.

A lot on your plate

In polite society having too much food piled on your plate is regarded as a sign of greed and possibly poor judgement, as recalled in the reprimand for leaving food uneaten on the plate, 'your eyes are bigger than your stomach'. There may be less an echo of censure when someone is said to have 'a lot on his plate', meaning he has too much to deal with and worry about.

A watched pot never boils

This mild reproof for signs of impatience is a reminder that nothing can be hastened by mere observation and anxiety. In the days when hungry families cooked all their meals in a single pot suspended over a fire, there must have been many 'watched pots' and many fraught cooks who resorted to this and similar expressions.

Above the salt

'Above the salt' recalls the importance given to salt in the Middle Ages, when it played a vital role in improving the taste of food of dubious quality. In wealthy households salt was given pride of place in the centre of the table, where a large salt cellar acted as a centre-piece. Only the most honoured guests and members of the household were invited to sit 'above the salt', that is nearer the top of the table than those who sat 'below the salt'. Both phrases have retained their social distinctions long after the segregation at table ceased.

Adam's ale

As the only drink available to the first man placed on earth by God, 'Adam's ale' is a euphemism for water. In Scotland it is sometimes referred to as 'Adam's wine'.

Adam's apple

To doctors, the protuberance in the front of the human throat, which is particularly prominent in men, is formed by the thyroid cartilage. Before the advent of modern medical science, folklore held that it was formed when a piece of the forbidden fruit (an apple), which Adam had eaten in the Garden of Eden, stuck in his throat.

After the meat mustard

Mustard eaten on its own is not very appetizing; taken with meat, however, mustard can enhance its flavour appreciably. This combination (or the lack of it) gave rise to the early saying 'after the meat mustard', alluding to the late arrival of something that would have been useful earlier but is now too late to be wanted.

All for heat and pilchards

A pilchard is a small fish related to the herring which is found around the coasts of south-west England, where this expression was coined. Warm, foggy weather in summer used to be described in Cornwall as 'all for heat and pilchards' implying that the sun would soon be breaking through with hot weather and that the shoals of pilchards would be gathering ready for the fishermen.

All hands and the cook

This unusual expression for a state of emergency was common in the cattle lands of the USA during the heyday of the cowboy in the second half of the nineteenth century. When the large herds of cattle became so restless that there was the risk of a stampede, every member of the team driving them north to market or the railhead, had to ride among them to quieten them down. This even applied to the cook, whose only usual duty on a cattle drive was to maintain a ready supply of food for the hungry hands.

All his geese are swans

By anyone's standards a mature swan is a more attractive bird than a goose and this expression of self-delusion rests on such a universal belief. Anyone who convinces himself that his children can do no wrong and that whatever he himself does is unmatchable in his own estimation can rightly be accused of believing that 'all his geese are swans'.

An apple a day keeps the doctor away

This well-known piece of dietary advice may be an early forerunner of the current belief among dieticians that our health can be approved by eating five portions of fresh fruit and vegetables a day. In 1866 a proverb from Pembrokeshire, quoted in *Notes & Queries*, ran, 'Eat an apple on going to bed, And you'll keep the doctor from earning his bread'. In *Rustic Speech* (1913) E.M. Wright quotes a West Country expression with similar meaning, 'Ait a happle avore gwain to bed, An' you'll make the doctor beg his bread.'

Apple of discord

An 'apple of discord' has meant a cause of dispute since ancient times. Greek legend holds that the goddess Eris (Discord) was furious at not being invited to the marriage of Thetis and Peleus, to which all the other gods and goddesses had been asked. During the wedding feast she threw onto the table a golden apple with the inscription 'for the fairest of them all.' Three goddesses vied for this and all tried to bribe Paris, who was picked to choose between them. Hera promised him wealth and power; Pallas Athena, military triumph; and Aphrodite, the love of the most beautiful woman in the world. Paris chose Aphrodite, who claimed the apple and later helped Paris seduce Helen, wife of the Greek warrior Menelaus, King of Sparta. This sparked off the Trojan war, in which the two slighted goddesses, Hera and Pallas Athene, helped to bring about the fall of Troy, Paris's home city to which he had taken Helen.

Apple of his (her) eye

In ancient biblical times the pupil of the eye was known as the 'apple of the eye' because it was believed to be a solid sphere, like an apple. The figurative use of the expression soon followed and was applied to anything that was held particularly dear, as indeed sight was. The phrase occurs in the Old Testament, notably in the reference to God's care of Jacob in Deuteronomy (XXXII.10), 'He kept him as the apple of his eye'. Today the expression is applied to any person or thing especially cherished.

Apple-pie bed

This expression may owe more to a French turn of phrase than to cooking apples. Making an 'apple-pie' bed is a practical joke in which the sheets are folded in such a way that it is impossible for anyone to get their legs down under the blankets. This may be derived from the French term *nappe pliée*, which means a 'folded sheet' or 'folded cloth'.

Apple-pie order

Once again expressions borrowed from French are the likely source of this popular turn of phrase rather than anything created in a kitchen. For anything to be in 'apple-pie order' implies that it is neat, perfectly arranged, with everything in its correct place. Two turns of phrase in French are possible candidates for its origin: *cap à pied* was a term used in the Middle Ages for a knight who was ready for battle and fully armed 'from head to foot'. Then there is the expression referred to above, *nappe pliée* meaning a 'folded cloth' or 'sheet'. Here too the sense is one of thorough tidiness and order.

As a pig loves marjoram

For as long as pigs have been kept as domestic animals it has been known that they have a strong aversion to any of the aromatic plants belonging to the marjoram family. So the expression 'as a pig loves marjoram' has come to mean an emphatic form of 'not at all'.

As thin as Banbury cheese

Banbury is a market town in the north of Oxfordshire associated with the Banbury Cross of nursery-rhyme fame, Banbury cakes, spiced turnovers that were originally made in the town, and Banbury cheese. The latter is a type of rich milk cheese which, in its finished state, is about an inch thick, in other words considerably slimmer than many other English cheeses. To be 'as thin as Banbury cheese' then, is to be very thin indeed.

Attic salt

Salt was a greatly esteemed commodity in the ancient world. As a seasoning sprinkled on food, it could greatly enhance the flavour. By analogy, 'salt' came to be used as a euphemism for 'wit', which sprinkled through conversation added sparkle and elegance to any gathering. Athenians were well-known for their wit and choice turns of phrase, and in time 'Attic salt' was applied to displays of elegant and well-chosen wit in any situation.

Bacon brains

Bacon was once the only meat available to English peasants and therefore references to 'bacon' were generally disparaging. 'Bacon brains' is another way of calling someone a 'simpleton', or a 'slow-witted yokel'.

Baker's dozen

Thirteen items make up a baker's dozen, one more than the traditional twelve. The practice and the expression date from times when bakers were subject to large fines if they sold bread that was underweight. To avoid this, they provided surplus loaves known as the 'inbread'. The thirteenth loaf in a baker's dozen was called the 'vantage loaf'.

Baker's knee

This is another term for 'knock-knee', the shape of the legs in which the knees bend inwards and knock together when walking. Popular belief held that bakers were especially prone to becoming knock-kneed, because of the position in which they had to stand for long periods while kneading bread.

Banana republic

If a country is described as a 'banana republic' the implication is less than flattering. 'Banana republics' are popularly perceived as small, Third World countries with fragile economies entirely dependent on the production of a single commodity, usually some kind of fruit. The original 'banana republics' were the small Caribbean and Central American states which were funded in the early part of the twentieth century by US corporations to develop the huge banana crop needed to supply the growing North American market. Once their prosperity and future growth were inextricably linked with growing and exporting bananas, they began to be referred to as 'banana republics'.

Barbecue

When Christopher Columbus led his first expedition to the Caribbean in 1492, he and his men encountered many new practices and customs. One of these was the method of cooking meat and fish on a framework of sticks and posts above a fire. The local word for this type of cooking was *barbacoa*, which that first Spanish expedition brought back to Europe when they returned. By the seventeenth century 'barbecue' had entered the English language and in due course the device on which food could be cooked outdoors was extended in meaning to include the social occasion at which such food was served.

Barley sugar

'Barley sugar' first acquired its unusual name from the French for 'burnt sugar' (*sucre brulé*), although it is now known in French as *sucre d'orge*; *orge* being the French for 'barley'.

Barmecide Feast

One of stories in the *Arabian Nights* tells of a prince of the great Barmecide family who played an unkind trick on a starving pauper by the name of Schacabac. The prince invited Schacabac to dine with him and then presented his guest with a succession of empty plates. As each was offered, the prince asked how Schacabac was enjoying his meal and to each enquiry the famished wretch replied politely in praise of the non-existent food. However, when he was offered imaginary wine, Schacabac saw his chance. Excusing himself by pretending to be drunk, he knocked the prince down. His host saw the funny side of his reaction, forgave him, and then served him with all the food and drink he could consume. From this story, a 'Barmecide Feast' has acquired the meaning of an illusion, notably one spiked with a great disappointment.

Basting your bacon

As bacon comes from the outside of a side of pork, it was the part most likely to be hit and 'basting your bacon' means to 'strike' or 'scourge'. In this context, 'basting' probably derived from the French word *bastiment* which was applied both to the pouring of fat over roasting meat and the beating of cloth. It is this latter meaning which is drawn on in 'basting your bacon'.

Beanfeast

A 'beanfeast' these days is a special outing or notable occasion which may or may not involve a meal and almost certainly has very little to do with beans. When the expression was coined, however, a 'beanfeast' was a highlight in the working calendar, the occasion once a year when an employer treated his employees to a feast. A bean goose was traditionally served at 'beanfeasts' held at the end of the year. These large grey birds arrive in England in the autumn and get their name from the bean-shaped mark on their bills. 'Beanfeasts' were also enhanced in days gone by with the serving of beans themselves.

Beans are in flower

It was once believed that the scent of bean flowers made people light-headed. As a result, commenting of someone that the 'beans are in flower' used to explain their silly behaviour.

Beef

This is one of several common words connected with food which shed interesting light on the social order that was established in England following the Norman Conquest. Saxons working as herdsmen for their Norman overlords referred to the animals in their charge as 'beef', from the Old French *boeuf*, meaning an 'ox', whereas the Normans enjoyed the cooked meat and used 'beef' to describe what had been roasted for them in the kitchens.

Beefcake

Beef has long been associated with strength and vigour. To put some 'beef' into something means to apply extra effort to it, hence the connection between 'beef' and muscularity. Photographs of powerfully-built male athletes and models have followed this line and are widely known by their admirers as 'beefcake'; the male counterpart to the earlier pin-up pictures of young women which were called 'cheesecake'.

Beefeater

The Yeoman Warders of the Tower of London have been known as 'beefeaters' since the middle of the seventeenth century. 'Eater' was once a synonym for a 'servant' and 'beefeaters' (servants who ate beef) were of higher rank than 'loafeaters', a term used for a 'menial servant'. There is a suggestion that the name may have originated from the French *buffetier*, which was the term given to servants who waited at the sideboard, but given the robust nature of a 'beefeater's' role in guarding the Tower of London, consuming beef seems a more plausible explanation of the name than serving from a sideboard.

Beefing

In American usage, 'beefing' carries the sense of 'complaining' and 'making an unnecessary fuss', which was coined from the underworld slang of London. The cry of the honest citizen 'stop thief, stop thief' was mocked by the rhyming slang of 'hot beef, hot beef' and from this 'beefing' came to mean 'making a fuss'.

Beer-money

Between 1800 and 1823 British soldiers and NCOs received a daily allowance of one penny in lieu of an issue of beer. The practice has long been forgotten, but 'beer-money' is still used to describe spare cash designated for spending on refreshments and treats.

Best thing since sliced bread

The automation of modern baking which produces millions of identical loaves of bread was regarded as a major advance in food production by both producers and consumers. The fact that these could be bought already sliced was thought an added bonus as it removed a boring chore. The US armed forces have been credited with coining 'the best thing since sliced bread' as a phrase of universal approval, which became widely used in the second half of the twentieth century.

Big Apple

New York City has been officially known as 'the Big Apple' for nearly thirty years, although the name was being applied to New York, along with several other large US cities, as long ago as the 1920s. One explanation rests on a jazz nightclub called the 'Big Apple', which was popular in the 1930s. Another puts forward the idea that the city's nickname stemmed from a popular dance called the Big Apple. Whatever the explanation, it probably lies in the nightclub or dance hall, where musicians hired to play in New York in the 1920s and 1930s knew that they had reached 'the big time'.

Big cheese

Although 'cheese' in this sense uses the same spelling as the food made from processed curds, that is as close as the two meanings come. A 'big cheese', meaning 'a important person', is derived from the Hindi word *chiz*, meaning the 'correct thing'. Its English derivative is probably a reference to the manner in which 'an important person', should be treated.

Boil down to

Since boiling reduces the volume of whatever is being boiled, this expression is a straightforward allusion to the cooking pot or kettle, in which something is reduced to its very essence; all extraneous material having been disposed of.

Bombay duck

'Bombay duck' is not a bird of any kind. It is a fish, known as a 'bummalo', which, dried and salted, is eaten as a relish with curry. The 'bummalo' is caught throughout South Asia, but its association with Bombay in this expression may stem from the Marathi name, *bombil*.

Boozing

These days 'boozing' is usually taken to be slang for drinking steadily and heavily. However, the history of the word shows that its pedigree reaches back to Middle English in which the verb *bousen* meant to 'drink deeply'. This was probably associated with the Dutch *buizen* and the German *bousen*, both meaning 'to drink to excess'.

Bottle up

'Bottling up' feelings and emotions means literally 'to hold them in control', 'to contain' them. The allusion is to the process of bottling preservatives and drinks, which enabled them to be set aside secure and undisturbed for a later date. At an appropriate opportunity, they could be 'unbottled' and the contents released, as circumstances and the occasion permitted.

Bread and butter

Describing something as 'bread and butter' these days, implies that it is in its most basic form; so a 'bread and butter' income is a basic income with no extras or additional benefits.

Breadwinner

'Bread', according to the old proverb, 'is the staff of life' and a 'breadwinner' is the provider of that staple commodity. The word is generally applied to the member of a family who supports the family financially.

Bringing home the bacon

For hundreds of years a pig was the sought-after prize at country fairs because pigs represented the only meat that many families ever ate. Bowling for a pig was a popular rural pastime enjoyed on feast days and other holidays, as was catching a greased pig. In both cases the winner was rewarded with a pig to take home and 'bringing home the bacon' became a popular euphemism for winning a prize, or succeeding in some form of contest.

Broaching your claret

In the boxing ring 'claret' was adopted as a word for 'blood' because of its dark red colour. In order to draw claret (or any other liquid) from a barrel, the barrel has to be 'broached' with a tap. So in boxing 'broaching your claret' came to mean 'giving you a bloody nose'.

Browse his jib

Aboard a sailing ship 'browsing the jib' meant hauling the jib sail taut; in other words making it tight. By association a sailor who made himself 'tight' through over-indulgence was said to have 'browsed his jib'. 'Jib' here refers to his face and 'browse' means 'to fatten'; an apt description of what happens when drinking too much results in a flushed and puffy face.

Bubble and squeak

A dish of cold boiled potatoes and green vegetables fried together was most likely given the name 'bubble and squeak' from the noise the ingredients supposedly made as they were being cooked. While being boiled, the potatoes and greens 'bubble' and, transferred to the pan, they 'squeak' as they fry in the fat.

Bully beef

'Bully beef' originated in the armed services where it became a principal component of naval and military rations towards the end of the nineteenth century. In the army 'bully beef' referred to tinned beef; in the Royal Navy it was the name given to boiled salt beef. Both are derived from the French for 'boiled beef' (*bouilli*, from the verb *bouillir* meaning 'to boil'); and *bouilli* was printed on the labels of tinned rations of beef supplied during the Franco-Prussian war of 1870–1.

Bunting

Any connection between the language of food and strings of flags hung up for high days and holidays may not be immediately apparent, until the material from which the flags were once made is taken into consideration. This was a strong gauzy woollen cloth, originally spun for sifting flour. In the West Country such sifting was known as 'bunting' and it seems likely that the material acquired this name even when it was put to other uses.

Butter

'Butter' has two immediate effects on plain bread: enhancing its flavour and covering it with a smooth surface. From these has developed the figurative use of 'butter' in phrases like 'to butter up', meaning to 'flatter' people and 'smooth' them down. The allusion to the smoothness and greasiness of 'butter' extends to the sporting field as well, where 'butterfingers' is a term of exasperation levelled at anyone who drops an easy catch.

Butter wouldn't melt in his mouth

One of the gastronomic delights of butter is its melting point, which is close enough the normal temperature of human beings that it melts when it is eaten, a process that adds to the flavour of whatever is being eaten with it. However, this is a process experienced and enjoyed by the eater alone; once inside the mouth, the butter and what happens to it is hidden from sight. Therefore anyone who gives the impression that 'butter wouldn't melt in his mouth' outwardly appears to be something which others know to be questionable; in other words, he seems to be too good to be true.

Buttering your bread on both sides

Both in action and meaning 'buttering your bread on both sides' indicates wasteful extravagance and luxury, which equates to a similar turn of phrase, 'having the best of both worlds'. In both senses, an individual 'buttering his bread on both sides' either seeks or achieves advantage from two sides at the same time.

Cabbage

Although the spelling is the same as that of the familiar green vegetable with a round heart, in the tailor's workshop 'cabbage' developed an entirely independent meaning from that in the greengrocer's shop or market garden. From the seventeenth century 'cabbage' was the term applied to pieces of cloth cut off by tailors and kept as a perk of the trade. As a result, tailors were sometimes nicknamed 'cabbages'. Outside the tailoring profession 'cabbage' acquired the broader meaning of 'pilfer', which links it with the Old French *cabas* meaning 'deceit' and 'theft', and the Dutch *kabassen,* 'to pilfer'.

Café au lait spots

'Café au lait' is made from mixing equal quantities of coffee and hot milk. The result is a hot drink, light-brown in colour. Its widespread popularity has led to the use of *café au lait* as the colour itself and by extension 'café au lait spots' is the term sometimes used to describe light-brown freckles.

Cafeteria

The first 'cafeteria' opened for business on 4 September 1885 on New Street in New York City. Called the Exchange Buffet, this was a self-service restaurant which led the way in developing a global market for what were to become 'fast-food' restaurants of every description. The name is derived from *cafetera*, Spanish for a 'maker or seller of coffee'.

Cakes and ale

Like 'beer and skittles', 'cakes and ale' is an expression that epitomizes the simple pleasures of life and one that has come to mean 'a good time' in general. In 1930 Somerset Maugham used it for the title of one of his novels.

Cat-lap

This was an old nickname given to any thin beverage, notably tea, which was current towards the end of the eighteenth century. The same genteel associations are found in 'catnap', a brief snooze while sitting, which originated in the middle of the nineteenth century.

Cellar

Used on its own these days, 'cellar' is generally taken to mean a 'wine cellar'. However, from the thirteenth century 'cellar' was applied to a 'store-room' housing a range of commodities; it was only a century later that it acquired the further definition as an 'underground store-room'. 'Cellar' in this sense is an English adaptation of the Old French *celier*, which was itself derived from the Latin for a 'store-room', *cella*. The other English use of the word, 'salt-cellar', is a corruption of the French *salière* meaning 'salt-dish'.

Cheesecake

In slang this is the female counterpart of 'beefcake': photographs of glamorous young women displaying their physical attractions before the camera. The term dates from the 1930s, though why 'cheesecake' should have been chosen as an appropriate description remains unclear. Perhaps the light, soft consistency of 'cheesecake' was deemed an appropriate analogy by men who bought the cards in the belief that the models pictured were 'light' and 'soft' themselves? Perhaps 'cheesecake' was a suitable companion to 'cupcake', another word given by male admirers to an attractive woman.

Cheesed off

'Cheesed off', like 'browned off' has meant 'fed up' and 'disgruntled' since the middle of the nineteenth century; there is a reference to 'cheese' in similar context in Dickens's novel *The Old Curiosity Shop*. When a 'cheese' goes 'off' it turns sour and loses its appeal. When heated, it turns brown as well. So 'cheesed off' and 'browned off' are closely related in both the culinary and figurative sense.

Cherry picking

Cherries have to be picked by hand and because of this a degree of selection can be involved in choosing the ripest and most succulent fruit. From the orchard this sense of selecting the best has passed into corporate life, where 'cherry picking' has become a widely used term in the context of 'asset-stripping.' Following a take-over or merger, the dominant partner in the deal may be accused of 'cherry-picking', if it selects the most profitable areas of the business and concentrates on maximizing profits from these at the expense of others which perform less well.

Chestnut

When 'chestnut' refers to a tired old joke that most listeners have heard before, it recalls a long-forgotten nineteenth-century melodrama, *The Broken Sword*, in which a character repeats the same jokes, with only a few small changes. In one scene he tells a joke involving a cork tree to another character, who interrupts to say that the tree was actually a 'chestnut'. He emphasizes the point by saying that he has heard the same joke twenty-seven times and is absolutely sure by now that the tree is a 'chestnut'. The expression was popularized in theatrical circles on both sides of the Atlantic and then passed into general use.

Chocolate

Since so much 'chocolate' is consumed today in its solid form, as confectionery, it is easy to forget that when it first came to Europe from Central America in the sixteenth century, 'chocolate' was served as a drink. The word has not changed since it arrived in England as a direct adoption of the Spanish *chocolate*. It was Spanish explorers who first came across 'chocolate' when they encountered the Aztec civilization in present-day Mexico. The Aztecs used cacao seeds to produce a type of food they called *chocolatl*. A similar sounding word, *cacaua-atl* was a drink made from cacao. Among the invaders from Europe the two were blended to produce *chocolate*, which came to refer to the produce of the cacao berry in both its solid and liquid state.

Chocolate-box

The first eating chocolate produced on a factory scale was manufactured in Vevey, Switzerland in 1819, by François-Louis Cailler. In 1842 John Cadbury began advertising 'French Eating Chocolate' in Great Britain, followed by Fry's first confectionery chocolate in 1853. It was not until 1875 that Daniel Peter, son-in-law of Mr Cailler, manufactured the first milk chocolate, once again in Vevey. By now the chocolate confectionery business was well-established, helped no doubt by the sentimental pictures which were chosen to decorate many 'chocolate boxes'. In 1868 Fry's chocolate assortment was packed in a box decorated with a picture of children in a goat-carriage. In the same year Richard Cadbury produced the first commercial design of what became known as 'chocolate-box art'. This was a portrait of his six-year-old daughter. These early examples set a pattern for ornate or overtly sentimental designs that came to epitomize 'chocolate-box' style and decoration.

Chowder

The eastern seaboard of North America was the home of 'chowder', the stew made from fish, notably clams. This probably owes its origin to fishermen from Brittany who settled in the area in order to fish the Grand Banks, the famous fishing grounds which lie south-east of Newfoundland. 'Chowder' came from the French *chaudière*, meaning a cooking pot, which occurred in the phrase *faire la chaudière*, that was common in the fishing villages of Brittany and referred to preparing a pot, with savoury condiments, in which a fish stew could be cooked.

Claret

'Claret' is an English word applied to red wines and these days to the wines of Bordeaux specifically. It was used originally to distinguish yellowish or light red wines from white wines. Today *clairet* in French refers to any local light red wine and in Old French *vin claret* was similarly applied to pale-coloured wines as distinct from white wines. English dropped the word *vin* ('wine') and made use of 'claret' alone when speaking of non-white wines.

Close as a Kentish oyster

For hundreds of years Kent has been renowned for the quality of its oysters. Since all oysters need to be tightly closed to ensure that they are good to eat, oysters from Kent were regarded as being shut tighter than most. So anything described as being 'close as a Kentish oyster' was similarly shut fast, from which developed its wider meaning of 'absolutely secret'

Cobbler

In the language of food and drink 'cobbler' is a word that may refer to both a fruit pie and a mixed drink. The origins of both are obscure. 'Cobbler' the drink is a blend of wine (usually sherry), sugar, lemon and crushed ice, which is taken through a straw. Its name may come from a slang use of 'cobble' meaning 'to patch up', in the sense that those who drank it finished 'patched up', in other words well and truly drunk. Another suggestion is that 'cobbler' is an abbreviation for 'cobbler's punch', a drink made from gin and water, to which treacle and vinegar were added. When it comes to 'cobbler' the pudding, its origin may be easier to pinpoint. This 'cobbler' is a deep fruit pie, topped with a crust similar to scone or plain cake dough which gives it the appearance of 'cobblestones' from which the name may have arisen.

Cocktail

About the only point of common agreement concerning the origin of 'cocktail' is that it was coined in the USA around 1800. On 13 May 1806 the American periodical *The Balance* contained this early reference, 'Cocktail is a kind of stimulating liquor, composed of spirits of any kind, sugar, water, and bitters – it is vulgarly called bitter sling and is supposed to be an excellent electioneering potion'. By that time *coquetel* was a popular mixed drink in the Gironde district of south-west France. Given the similarity of name and contents, this seems as plausible an explanation of the origin of 'cocktail' as any other.

Codswallop

To describe an idea or suggestion as 'codswallop' is summarily to dismiss it as stupid nonsense, especially when it is offered as serious information or instruction. This sense has developed some way from the original meaning of 'codswallop' when it was coined in the late nineteenth century as the nickname for mineral water and other soft drinks. In 1875 Hiram Codd developed a new kind of mineral water bottle which used a marble as a stopper. His surname was added to the slang for beer ('wallop') to create 'Codd's wallop', the disparaging term among drinkers for all non-alcoholic drinks. As the expression became more widely used, the spelling changed to 'codswallop' and the meaning was broadened to include anything dismissed as 'rubbish'.

Coffee

'Coffee' first arrived in Europe from southern Arabia, via Turkey, so it is natural that its name in various European languages should reflect its point of origin. In fact 'coffee', *café* in French and *caffé* in Italian, comes from the Turkish *kahveh*, which in turn came from the Arabic for 'coffee', *qahwah*.

Cold fish

Anyone lacking in warm feelings or appearing unemotional and impassive could be described as a 'cold fish', following the widely-held conviction that all fish are cold-blooded and therefore incapable of feeling.

Colonial goose

This is an Australian dish developed on sheep stations to vary the unrelenting diet of plain mutton. In preparation it has nothing to do with a goose. Instead it comprises a boned leg of mutton, stuffed with breadcrumbs, herbs and onion before being roasted.

Condiments

'Condiments' used to season and flavour food have been known in English since the fifteenth century. The English word comes directly from Latin, in which *condimentum* carries the same meaning.

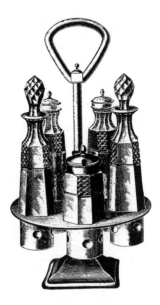

Cooking the books

Falsifying accounts is colloquially referred to as 'cooking the books', perhaps because changing the figures to create a set of results that suits a particular purpose is similar to the art of taking basics foodstuffs and transforming them into something different and more appealing by means of 'cooking'.

Cooking your goose

The tradition of eating goose in autumn may have something to do with the obscure origin of this phrase. Goose was served at Michaelmas (29 September) when autumn was well under way and winter fast approaching. In days gone by this would have heralded long months in which whatever food there was would become increasingly scarce and less palatable. Perhaps 'cooking your goose', which means 'ruining your chances' and 'making a fatal mistake', carries the sense of consuming the last of the palatable food. 'Cooking someone else's goose' has the similar meaning of 'ruining their plans'.

Cool as a cucumber

Cucumbers have been known to maintain a cool temperature since they were first cultivated in ancient times and it may not be an accident that they were first extensively propagated in the hot climates of India and the Near East. This characteristic has led to the popular synonym 'as cool as a cucumber' when referring to someone who remains perfectly composed in all circumstances.

Couch potato

Tempting as it is to see the shape of the potato as a key element in this popular turn of phrase, its history suggests that it may be coincidental. The 'couch potato' was first given his name in America in the late 1970s, in recognition of those who spend too long slumped in front of a television rather than taking part in other forms of entertainment or exercise. In America 'boob tube' is slang for a television set and it may be the pun on 'tube/tuber' that was responsible for the 'potato' association in the phrase. In some cases 'couch potatoes' may well be potato-shaped, but this does not appear to be a prerequisite in qualifying for the classification.

Crackers

This is an abbreviation for the expression 'crack-brained', meaning, as the wording suggests, 'slightly mad' or 'eccentric' and is nothing to do with the biscuits customarily eaten with cheese today.

Cry barley

'Barley' in this usage is a variant of 'parley', the cry for truce in rough-and-tumble games enjoyed for hundreds of years. 'Cry Barley' was itself the name of a country game, similar to 'Prisoner's Base', in which players made use of a 'home' called 'hell'.

Cup of cha

'Cha' is the anglicized form of the Mandarin Chinese word for 'tea'. Its use in English is first recorded early in the seventeenth century and since then a 'cup of cha' has become widely used as an alternative to a 'cup of tea'. A similar word occurs in several

Indian languages and the adoption of these during the British rule of India helped to popularize the expression.

Curate's egg

A cartoon in *Punch* magazine dating from 1895 gave rise to the expression 'good in parts, like the curate's egg.' In the cartoon a nervous young curate, seated at his bishop's breakfast table, is addressed by his lordship who says, 'I'm afraid you've got a bad egg, Mr Jones!' The curate, desperate not to offend, replies, 'Oh no, my Lord, I assure you! Parts of it are excellent!' From this, 'good in parts, like the curate's egg', has come to describe something 'patchy' and of 'uneven quality'.

Cutting the mustard

'Cutting the mustard' is one of several popular expressions which are generally used in a negative sense; as such it refers to a failure to reach a desired standard, as in 'He's not cutting the mustard'. Its origin is obscure. One belief is that 'mustard' is linked with the military term 'pass muster', which means to 'measure up'. Another explanation looks at the creation of 'mustard' itself, in which the addition of vinegar reduces, or 'cuts', the bitter taste of mustard seed. Maybe the use of mustard to develop and improve the flavour of food lies at the root of the expression? Whatever its origin, failing to 'cut the mustard' is tantamount to 'failure' itself.

Different as chalk and cheese

Chalk and cheese share a superficial similarity of appearance, in that chalk and a good many cheeses are white and fine-grained. Beyond that the two are poles apart. So the phrase 'different as chalk and cheese' is an emphatic statement of difference.

Dining with the cross-legged knights

To 'dine with the cross-legged knights' is to go without any dinner at all. The 'crossed-legged knights' referred to were the stone effigies of Templar knights in the Temple Church in London, which later became a meeting place for lawyers and their clients. This was also the haunt of layabouts who frequented the Temple on the off chance of being hired as witnesses.

Dish up spurs

During the Middle Ages the border separating England from Scotland was the scene of local vendettas and guerilla campaigns. Scottish raiders invariably returned home with rustled English cattle, on which the chieftain's household fed. When supplies of beef began to run low, the lady of the household would send up a pair of spurs as the last course, to show her menfolk that it was time to don their spurs and carry out another raid south of the border to replenish the laird's larder.

Doing porridge

This is slang for 'spending time in prison', which terminology increased in popularity with the success of the 1970s situation comedy, *Porridge*, that dealt with life in prison. Its origin is said to be from the rhyming slang 'borage and thyme', meaning 'time', with reference to a prisoner's term behind bars. It should also be remembered that 'porridge' was once a staple food in prison.

Don't count your chickens before they are hatched

'Don't count your chickens before they are hatched' is a long-established warning not to make, or act on, an assumption which may turn out to be wrong, even if the prospects appear to be favourable. The proverb is based on Aesop's fable about a milkmaid who was so preoccupied with the eggs she was going to buy with the proceeds from her milk, that she lost concentration and spilt the pail of milk that would have provided the wherewithal for the eggs.

Don't put all your eggs in one basket

Although this well-known caution first appeared in print in an Italian book of proverbs published in 1662, it had probably been in use long before that. The warning is clear: 'don't chance everything on a single venture, but spread the risk'.

Done to a turn

Here is a phrase, still used in modern cookery, which dates from the medieval kitchen where joints and other meat were cooked on a spit above the fire. To ensure that everything was cooked evenly, the spit was slowly rotated, exposing each face of the meat to an equal amount of heat. Meat that was 'done to a turn' was cooked exactly right; one more turn on the spit would have overcooked it. Away from the kitchen, 'done to a turn' refers to other activities that are satisfactorily completed.

Doughboy

During the mid-nineteenth century American infantry uniforms were fastened with large brass buttons. In the eyes of many people these resembled a type of pastry originally cooked for sailors. Thus the name moved from pastry dough, to infantry button, to the soldier himself, creating 'doughboy' as a nickname for the American infantryman for years to come.

Drinking a toast

An old custom demanded that toast should be put into tankards of beer to improve their flavour. Strange as this appears, it is no more bizarre than the story in a very early edition of the *Tatler*, which introduced the practice of drinking 'toasts' as a compliment to individuals or institutions. The story goes that during the reign of Charles II, a renowned beauty was in the Cross Bath at Bath, when one of her admirers took a glass of the water in which she was standing and drank her health to all present. This prompted another gentleman, who had been indulging in stronger drink than water, to exclaim that he would jump in the water, for, 'though he liked not the liquor, he would have the toast', in other words the lady herself. Thereafter, compliments expressed publicly and accompanied by a drink became known as 'toasts'.

Drinking at Freeman's Quay

Anyone 'drinking at Freeman's Quay' is enjoying a drink at someone else's expense. However, although there is a Freeman's Quay near London Bridge, where, it is said, porters and carmen who called received a free pot of beer, the euphemistic use of 'Freeman's' seems a more likely origin for the expression.

Drop like a hot potato

Since a considerable quantity of a potato's mass is comprised of water, it retains heat very effectively and is capable of burning fingers that touch it too eagerly after it is removed from the oven. By analogy, a 'hot potato' has come to mean a situation or predicament that is 'too hot to handle'. Similarly to drop something 'like a hot potato' means to get rid of it very quickly, before it harms you or your interests.

Drowning the miller

Even millers whose livelihoods depend on a constant flow of water to turn the waterwheels of their mills would be overwhelmed by the volume of water alluded to in 'drowning the miller'. The hyperbole is amusing when applied to an excessive amount of water added to spirits, or tea, which dilutes them to the point of being almost tasteless and scarcely worth drinking.

Drunk as blazes

In this expression 'blazes' refers to the 'devil' or 'hell'; therefore to be 'drunk as blazes' is to be very drunk indeed. It is possible that a similar meaning may be due to a corruption of 'blaiziers', referring to guild members who enthusiastically threw themselves into the drinking and revelry that honoured St Blaize, the patron saint of wool-combers.

Earn your salt

In ancient Rome soldiers used to be paid an allowance to buy salt, which was known as *salarium* (*sal* being the Latin for 'salt'). This is the origin of 'salary' and anyone who earns their 'salt' therefore earns their 'salary'.

Easy as pie

The reference here is more than likely to eating a pie rather than making one, since 'easy as pie' refers to anything that is ridiculously simple.

Eating Dunmow bacon

Old tradition in Dunmow in Essex held that any person who could honestly swear (and prove) that for the previous twelve months and a day he or she had never had a row with their spouse and never wished themselves unmarried, could claim a side of bacon, known as a flitch. The tradition of the Dunmow Flitch dates from the twelfth century and 'eating Dunmow bacon' is a well-established term for a happily married life.

Eating the leek

In Shakespeare's *Henry V* the Welsh captain, Fluellen, is affronted by Pistol's insults directed at the leek he proudly wears in his cap, to the point where his anger boils over and he beats Pistol until he eats the leek, leaves and all. In allusion to this, 'to eat the leek' means being forced 'to eat your words', or 'take back' something you have said.

Egg on

The 'egg' referred to here is an Old Norse word for the sharp side of a blade. This makes the sense of 'egg on', meaning to 'urge' and 'encourage' easier to understand. Anyone 'encouraged' by the cutting edge of a sword or dagger is more than likely to comply with what is requested. Used in this context, 'egg' is thought to be related to the Latin *acies*, meaning 'sharpness' as well as 'the edge of a blade'; *acus* a 'thorn' or 'needle' in Latin has a similar origin.

Egg-trot

Riding with a load of eggs carried in panniers required a steady gait to avoid breaking the shells, so 'egg-trot' came into being for a cautious jog-trot pace that avoided any undue shocks or exertion.

Egghead

An 'egghead' in slang is a 'highbrow' or 'intellectual', by association with someone who is bald; baldness and intellectual qualities going hand in hand in this context. Since baldness results in a smooth domed scalp similar to an egg shell, a bald person became known as an 'egghead'.

Eggs is eggs

Here is another instance of 'egg' being misapplied in a commonly used expression. In this case the 'eggs' in question owe more to mathematics than to hens. The phrase 'as sure as eggs is eggs' means 'completely safe' and 'absolutely certain'. Both carry the sense of irrefutable logic which is regularly found in mathematics, which leads to the general assumption that the expression originated in the mathematical statement 'as sure as x is x'.

Every bean has its black

An old Roman saying, 'every bean has its own black' refers to the black 'eye' found in many beans and carries the meaning that 'each of us has our own faults'.

Fiasco

Today a 'fiasco' is such a familiar expression for a 'failure' or 'breakdown' in general that its earlier connection with a dramatic or musical performance is frequently overlooked. However, the origin of that association is even more obscure, stemming as it does from *fiasco* the Italian for a 'bottle', in the sense of the English 'flask'. The allusion to disaster, or a bad performance is hard to fathom. Perhaps a poor glass blower had a 'fiasco' when he burst a bottle he was making? Maybe the story of an Italian actor who failed to raise the laughs he was expecting on stage and loudly blamed the bottle he was using, helped to spread 'fiasco' in the usage to which we now put it?

Fine words butter no parsnips

At one time parsnips were more widely eaten than they are today and by tradition they were served with butter to enhance their flavour. 'Fine words butter no parsnips' is an old saying recorded from the early seventeenth century. It appears in various versions, all with the same meaning: that words alone will not feed a family.

Fine kettle of fish

A 'fine kettle of fish' (sometimes a 'pretty kettle of fish') means a 'muddle', or a 'messy business' and refers to the riverside picnic of the same name which forms a part of the traditional salmon fishing season in parts of Scotland. In this 'kettle of fish', freshly caught salmon are immediately put into a pot of boiling water right on the river bank. As soon as the fish are cooked, they are eaten by hand. Delicious as the result may be, the process is understandably messy, which accounts for its association with an unfortunate predicament.

Fish out of water

To behave like a 'fish out of water' is to appear ill at ease away from your familiar environment. The allusion to a fish floundering on land or the deck of a fishing-boat has been used since ancient times and is still current.

Fishwife

Fish, above almost all other foods, need to be sold fresh. In days gone by it was common for a fisherman's wife to take her husband's most recent catch to market. There she did her utmost to make sure that everything was sold before any of the fish started to turn bad. This required her to hawk her wares loudly and with increasing vehemence as the day wore on. So the term 'fishwife' came to be applied to any loud, coarse-mannered woman.

Flapjack

Flat oat cakes, baked on a griddle or in a shallow pan, were called 'flapjacks' because, like pancakes, they were once turned by being tossed in the air. In the course of this their shape must have resembled the flapping of a bird's wing.

Flat as a pancake

'Pancakes' are thin cakes of batter, fried on both sides on a griddle or in a frying-pan. The batter from which a pancake is made usually contains a high level of liquid which spreads out across the pan as it is poured in. As a result the cooked pancake is flat and thin, giving rise to the expression as 'flat as a pancake', meaning very flat indeed.

Flavour of the month

Competition in the ice-cream business in America led to ice-cream parlours across the country promoting their business by featuring a special 'flavour of the month', often at a reduced price to attract custom. By the 1980s the phrase had come to describe anything or anyone temporarily in vogue.

Forbidden fruit

The earliest reference to the first 'forbidden fruit' comes in the second chapter of the Book of Genesis, when God warns Adam, the first man, 'Of every tree of the garden thou mayest freely eat: But of the tree of the knowledge of good and evil, thou shalt not eat of it: for in the day that thou eatest thereof thou shalt surely die'. From this 'forbidden fruit' has come to mean 'forbidden' or 'unlawful pleasure' of any kind, particularly illicit love.

Forking out

From the late seventeenth century 'the forks' was slang for the middle and fore fingers. This was probably because of their shape and the purpose they served in the underworld of 'digging' into other people's pockets and purses. From this usage the expression 'forking out' came to mean 'handing over' or 'paying up'.

Four-ale bar

At one time the cheapest beer sold for fourpence a quart, which equated to twopence a pint (less than a penny a pint in decimal currency). From this, public bars, where the cheapest beer was sold, became known as 'four-ale bars'.

French cream

This became a euphemism for 'brandy' following the French custom of adding a glass of brandy to an after-dinner cup of coffee in place of cream.

Fritter away

Although the spelling of 'fritter' is identical in both its common uses, the two words have no other association. The 'fritter' that is a portion of batter fried in oil is ultimately derived from the Latin *frigere*, meaning 'to fry'. However, when the same spelling is applied to 'fritter away', in the sense of 'waste' and 'squander', its origin is related to 'fritters', which was recorded from the seventeenth century with the meaning of 'fragments'.

Fudge

'Fudge', like 'fritter' above, occurs in English with two distinct meanings. The most recent, dating from the second half of the nineteenth century is the familiar confectionery made from chocolate, sugar and milk. When 'fudge' is used as a verb, as in 'fudging' an issue, the meaning and origin are older. By the seventeenth century 'fudge' was used in the sense of 'patching up' and 'faking', which stemmed from the Middle English *fage*, meaning to 'deceive' and 'beguile'.

Full of beans

'Full of beans' was once used of a horse that was full of energy and in tip-top condition. What part 'beans' had to play in the animal's form is unclear; perhaps beans were equated with energy and vitality? By the nineteenth century 'full of beans' had moved from horses to humans and people were similarly being described as being 'full of beans' if they too were in 'good form' and showing every sign of being in 'high spirits'.

Getting your teeth into

'Getting your teeth into' something is a matter of literally 'getting to grips with it'. Whether you are 'getting your teeth into' a piece of work, a difficult problem, or a challenge of some sort, the allusion in this popular turn of phrase is to start 'chewing' and 'gnawing' at it in a determined and resolute manner.

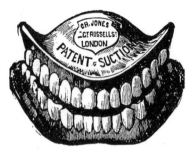

Gilt off the gingerbread

Until the middle of the nineteenth century stalls selling 'gingerbread' were a common sight at fairs throughout the country. The 'gingerbread' was a cake mixed with treacle and flavoured with spices. It was often cut into shapes, such as 'gingerbread men', and it was common for it to be decorated with gold leaf, or 'gilt'. This was sometimes genuine gold leaf, but in most cases it was imitation. Taking the 'gilt off the gingerbread' revealed what it really was, which gave rise to the wider meaning of the expression: showing something up as worth far less than imagined and, by association, destroying an illusion.

Gin

The distinctive taste of gin comes from the juice of juniper berries used to flavour it. Juniper also helped establish the name 'gin' as the one by which the spirit is now commonly known. In Old French the word for 'juniper' was *genevre* (*genièvre* in modern French). In English this became known as 'Geneva' which was abbreviated by the eighteenth century to 'gin'.

Ginger up

The hot, spicy flavour that ginger lends to anything it is added to, has resulted in its use as a verb. The act of 'gingering up' someone means provoking them into activity, often by arousing anger and thereby raising their temperature.

Give the cold shoulder

The original 'cold shoulder' in this well-used turn of phrase was a rather bland 'cold shoulder' of mutton, which a host would produce for a guest who had outstayed his welcome. On arrival the guest would customarily have been treated to an appetizingly hot roast joint. The cold shoulder, by contrast, was less appealing and a none too subtle sign that it was time to leave. The meaning has subsequently extended beyond the code of hospitality. In its wider sense, 'giving the cold shoulder' means 'assuming a distant manner' which makes it clear that you want nothing to do with a particular individual.

Giving a basting

This is another use of 'basting' in the sense of 'giving a bashing' or 'beating'. It is possible that it may derive from the practice of medieval cooks beating lazy scullions with the 'basting stick' used to pour hot fat from the dripping pan over the joint and other meat roasting on the spit.

Giving beans

'Giving beans' to someone means to 'give [them] a thrashing'. This is an old expression which may be a straightforward translation of the French *S'il me donne des poids, je lui donnerai de fèves*, meaning 'If he gives me peas, I'll give him beans'. The sense is similar to the expression 'to return [something] with interest', in other words to repay blows with an even stronger buffeting.

Go bananas

During the twentieth century 'going bananas' became widely used for 'going crazy' or 'excited', often with violent repercussions. Why 'bananas' should be credited with this effect is uncertain. The apparent instability of 'banana republics' may have had an influence. In Australia and America 'banana oil' was used colloquially for 'nonsense'. There is also the suggestion that the curved shape of the banana, which deviated from the 'straight' line may have been an influence, just as 'pear-shaped' has become a popular way of referring to something that has gone badly wrong.

Going to Tommy Dodd for drinks

'Tommy Dodd' in this expression is the 'odd man out', the one who loses the toss of a coin and drops out of a group. There may be several 'Tommy Dodds' in a group at the start, but in the end only two men are left tossing the coin to see who will pay for a round of drinks. So 'going to Tommy Dodd for drinks' really means 'tossing a coin to see who will pay for the next round'.

Gone to pot

In earlier times it was common to keep a pot over the fire into which left-overs were put to be cooked and served up as a hash. Pieces of meat and vegetables that could not be used in any other dish ended up in the pot and this practice gave rise to 'gone to pot' meaning 'ruined' or 'no longer of use'.

Gooseberry fool

'Gooseberry fool' is a dish made from gooseberries, sugar and cream or custard, in which the gooseberries are crushed through a sieve. In this sense 'fool' is an adaptation of the French *fouler*, 'to crush'.

Grapes of wrath

John Steinbeck took this as the title for his 1939 Pulitzer Prize-winning novel about the plight of dispossessed Oklahoma farming families forced to leave the Dust Bowl to seek another life in the west. Before him Julia Ward Howe had made good use of it in her famous Civil War song, the 'Battle Hymn of the American Republic', which she composed in December 1861:

> Mine eyes have seen the glory of the coming of the Lord:
> He is trampling out the vintage where the grapes of wrath are stored.

But they both owe a debt to the author of the Book of Revelations, who wrote at the end of the fourteenth chapter:

> And the angel thrust in his sickle into the earth, and gathered the vine of the earth, and cast it into the great winepress of the wrath of God.
>
> And the winepress was trodden without the city, and blood came out of the winepress, even unto the horse bridles, by the space of a thousand and six hundred furlongs.

Grapevine

News carried on the 'grapevine' these days tends to be hearsay and rumour, whereas the original use of the 'grapevine' was to signal a definite message. The expression was coined in America at the time when the abolition of slavery was gathering momentum. Supporters of abolition used laundry hung on a clothes-line to signal the security situation in their neighbourhood. One selection of clothes and other laundry signalled that it was safe for runaway slaves to move in the area; a different selection showed that it was dangerous. Since rope was expensive, 'grapevines' were often substituted as clothes-lines and so the primitive signalling system became known as the 'grapevine telegraph', later shortened to the 'grapevine' on its own.

Greengage

In 1725, or thereabouts, Sir William Gage of Hengrove in Suffolk introduced a variety of green plum into England from France. This was named in his honour, the 'greengage'.

Grog

Until a couple of hundred years ago officers and men in the Royal Navy were issued with regular supplies of neat rum. This may have helped to improve morale but it did little to improve efficiency and discipline. In 1740 Admiral Vernon, who was then Commander-in-Chief West Indies, began issuing watered-down rum to the men under his command. The admiral was nicknamed Old Grog because of the cloak he habitually wore, which was made from grogram, a coarse material spun from silk and wool and stiffened with gum. Before long the daily drink ration he had introduced acquired the same nickname and in time 'grog' became more widely applied to all kinds of alcoholic drink. The effects of over-indulgence in Admiral Vernon's creation and similar drinks led to the creation of 'groggy', which was well established by the nineteenth century in the sense of 'shaky' and 'tottering', and can refer to weakness due to illness not solely the result of too much alcohol.

Guinea fowl

The only connection between these birds and the 'guinea' coin distributed in England, is that both the gold from which the coin was minted and the bird came from Guinea in West Africa.

Guns before butter

'Guns before butter' was a political catchphrase that has become closely associated with the Nazi leadership in Germany in the 1930s. Goebbels, Goering and Hess all made use of it in one form or another, insisting that Germany needed to be strongly armed rather than treated to the luxuries of life. The phrase has been quoted subsequently in situations in which a country, placed on a war footing, has had to forsake even simple pleasures in the interests of national defence.

Half a loaf is better than no bread

There are many proverbs urging us to make the best of our lot and this one was quoted by John Heywood in his *Dialogue of Proverbs* in 1546. The meaning is plainly that if you can't get all that you want, you should try to be content with what you do manage to get; after all, something is better than nothing.

Half-baked

Anything 'half-baked' is, by allusion to the bread oven, 'soft', 'unfinished' and 'incomplete'. As a consequence the term is widely used in the case of individuals whom some might describe as being 'soft in the head'. 'Half-baked' is also applied to propositions and ideas regarded as 'ill-conceived' and 'not fully thought through'.

Ham actor

Ham actors have strutted on the stage since the days of Shakespeare, indeed there is a scene in *Hamlet* when the prince gives the visiting players a few tips on how to avoid being 'ham actors'. It is possible that the first three letters of *Hamlet* may provide one possible explanation for the origin of 'ham actor'; both because of the prince's thorough account of a 'ham actor's' gestures and style of delivery and for the stage tradition that all has-beens on the stage played Hamlet at some earlier stage in their careers. Another line of thought focuses on 'ham fat' as a possible origin for 'ham actor'. In the nineteenth-century theatre some actors removed their make-up with 'ham fat'. There was also an old-style of black-face comic whose make-up comprised ham fat dusted with burnt cork. Such a 'ham-fatter' was looked down on by everyone else on the stage. The origin of the 'ham actor' may be uncertain, but few would argue that Hamlet's description is as appropriate today as it was four hundred years ago.

Hamburger

'Beefburger' is a word coined in the food preparation and catering industry in the lame attempt to avoid the unlikely confusion between 'beef' and 'ham' in the 'hamburger'. The universal availability of 'hamburgers' today ensures that everyone who eats them surely knows that the flat cake of fried meat and onion is made from beef not ham. The 'hamburger' acquired its name in America because it was first brought to the New World by sailors from the north-west German port of Hamburg, around which beef had been prepared and eaten in this form for several hundred years.

Ham-fisted

To be 'ham-fisted' is to be 'clumsy'. The expression no doubt refers to large hands which are shaped like hams and are therefore less than ideal for dextrous manual tasks.

Hard cheese

'Hard cheese' meaning 'tough luck' has a distinctive nineteenth-century ring and was common among the officer class of the Victorian army. The allusion is obscure, though the unpalatable nature of cheese that has gone hard, may convey something of the disappointment and sense of bad luck implicit in the phrase.

Hash

'Hash' is a dish made from left-overs: chopped up meat, potatoes and vegetables mixed together and cooked in a pan. It is a lowly meal and as such has influenced the use of 'hash' in phrases like 'to make a hash of' something, meaning to 'make a mess' of it.

He eats no fish

This was a term current during the reign of Elizabeth I and meant that the man referred to was 'honest' and 'trustworthy'. Such an assertion was based the grounds that he did not eat fish on Fridays, an action which distinguished Roman Catholics from Protestants, who refused to follow what was widely regarded as a Papist superstition.

Here we go gathering nuts in May

Since there are no nuts that can be gathered in May, this old children's rhyme is another example of how two words that sound similar can be confused. The line originally ran 'Here we go gathering knots of may', which referred to the time-honoured custom of gathering 'knots' of flowers on May Day.

High tea

'High tea' is an early evening meal that is more substantial than, and therefore elevated above, the afternoon 'tea' of dainty sandwiches and cakes, but offering less to eat than supper, which is served later in the evening.

Honeymoon

The first thirty days of marriage was literally a period of 'sweetness' for followers of an old Germanic custom which required the newly married couple to drink diluted honey during their first month of life together. This was later supplemented with mead (a sweet wine made from honey). Honeymoons were not, and are not, restricted to Germanic peoples, however. French couples begin their life together with a *lune de miel* ('moon of honey') as do their Italian counterparts who enjoy a *luna di miele*.

Hooch

'Hooch' was coined in America as the slang for 'rough whisky', or other crudely distilled spirits. The word is an abbreviation of the Alaskan Indian *hoochino*, the name of the tribe that brewed a liquor of this sort.

Horseradish

The use of 'horse' as a prefix often denotes a coarseness, or large size as in: 'horse chestnut', 'horseplay' and 'horse laugh'. 'Horse-radish' has a larger and more pungent root than the normal radish. This explains why it tends to be used to make a piquant sauce, often served with beef, rather than being eaten in its entirety like the ordinary radish, which is a common ingredient in salads.

Hot cross bun

By tradition the spiced fruit buns baked for Good Friday were marked with a cross as a sign that they had been made supposedly from the same dough used to bake the bread of the holy Eucharist. The sacred nature of 'hot cross buns' apparently accounted for the belief that they would keep for a year without showing signs of mould and it used to be common practice to hang one or more in a house to ward off evil spirits. Today's all-year-round mass-produced versions have, to a large extent, lost any religious significance.

Hot dog

It appears that 'hot dogs' did not acquire their now universally recognized name until the beginning of the twentieth century. Hot sausages served in long rolls or buns had been sold by street vendors in America during the nineteenth century. Long sausages known as 'frankfurters' after the German city where they had originated, were particularly popular. Since their shape also resembled the long-bodied, short-legged German dog called a dachshund, the sausages became known as 'hot dachshund sausages', which proved to be a bit of mouthful in every respect. It was the sports cartoonist T.A. Dorgan, known to his fans as TAD, who took the final step and started referring to the hot sausage in a roll as a 'hot dog' and almost immediately the name superseded all others.

Hotchpotch

Two French words *hocher* ('to shake') and *pot* ('pot') provide the source for 'hotchpotch' in both its culinary and legal meanings. By the fifteenth century 'hotchpotch' was the name given to a thick broth made from a mixture of ingredients: meat, vegetables, condiments and anything else the cook cared to add. This gave rise to the wider meaning, in which a 'hotchpotch' is a 'confused jumble'. As a legal term 'hotchpotch' is a process involved with the division of a fund or estate between a number of beneficiaries. If one of them has already received a share, he or she may be asked to bring that share into 'hotchpotch', in other words to have it taken into consideration as part of the total fund, before individual shares can be apportioned.

How many beans make five

Everyone 'knows how many beans make five'; the answer obviously is 'five'. However, this leads into the trick question 'But how many blue beans make five white beans?' The implication behind this being that only the sharp-witted will produce the right answer. In time the expression has been abbreviated to its current form; anyone who knows 'how many beans make five' is 'no fool'. And the answer? Five blue beans make five white ones – if they are peeled.

Humble pie

The food served at a medieval hunting feast marked a clear social distinction between the diners. At high table the lord, his family and guests were served venison, while further down the table the huntsmen and retainers were given the deer's entrails, or 'umbles', made into a pie. 'Humble pie' is a pun on 'umble pie' and anyone presented with it is required to eat inferior food in an inferior position. Therefore those made to 'eat humble pie' have to come down from a lofty position to which they have elevated themselves, in order to defer to others and often be humiliated by people they had previously looked down on.

I have eggs on the spit

Cooking eggs on a spit was a particularly time-consuming process in medieval cookery which required the cook's constant attention. First the eggs had to be boiled, then the yolks were removed to be mixed with spices, before being replaced inside the whites. Following this, they were fed onto a spit and roasted over the fire. With so much to attend to, the cook had no time for anything else, which gave rise to the current use of the expression; 'I have eggs on the spit' means 'I am too busy to do anything else'.

I should cocoa

'I should cocoa' is less frequently used today than it once was, though its meaning remains 'certainly not!' The origin of the curious expression lies in rhyming slang, from which 'cocoa' is related to 'coffee and cocoa', meaning 'I should hope so!' used ironically to mean the exact opposite.

If you can't stand the heat, get out of the kitchen

Plain-speaking Harry S. Truman, the thirty-third president of the United States who held office from 1945 until 1953, coined a number of memorable down-to-earth maxims, of which this became one of the most widely used. As he wrote in *Mr Citizen*, published in 1960, 'I used to have a saying that applies here, and I note the some people have picked it up: "If you can't stand the heat, get out of the kitchen."' The allusion to slaving over a hot stove, while under pressure to prepare a meal, is well applied to other situations in the sense of 'if you can't take the strain, don't get involved'.

In a jam

Although spelt the same as the conserve of fruit boiled to a pulp, which we know as 'jam', the word in this expression has been recorded since the eighteenth century in the sense of 'to press' or 'squeeze tightly'. As a noun, a 'jam' in this context is the result of being 'pressed' or 'squeezed', usually into a situation that is not of one's choosing.

In a pickle

References to being 'in a pickle' date back to the time of William Shakespeare and all are applied with the sense of being 'in a predicament' or 'in a sorry plight'. From the fourteenth century a 'pickle' was a brine in which food was preserved. Perhaps the unpleasant taste of this salt liquor led to the origin of the phrase which has been current for over four hundred years.

In a stew

The allusion of 'a state of anxiety' to being 'in a stew' dates from nineteenth-century slang. This may be due to the agitated state in which the contents of a stew are cooked combined with the perspiration that can be caused when people 'in a stew' become over-heated.

In meal or in malt

The reference here is to grain production and milling, both of which were capable of producing a profit. 'In one way or another', or figuratively 'in meal or malt', the miller would benefit since he was entitled to a share of the proceeds, whether the grain was used to produce 'meal' or 'malt'.

It's no use crying over spilt milk

In 1659 this proverb was recorded as 'No weeping for shed milk' and it is likely that it was in use long before that. The allusion to the dairy and kitchen is self-evident: milk, once spilt, is wasted and cannot be retrieved. In the same way, once a misfortune has occurred it cannot be remedied. We might also say, that 'you can't turn back the clock'.

Jerked beef

'Jerked beef' consists of beef cut into strips and dried in the sun. The term entered English in the eighteenth century as the anglicized form of the South American word *charqui* for meat preserved in the same way.

Junket

'Junket' started life in the fourteenth century as a rush basket for carrying fish. By the following century it had become a dish prepared with curdled cream which was laid on a bed of rushes.

A century later 'junket' had moved upmarket to become a dainty dish or confection served at feasts and banquets. From there it was only a short move to apply 'junket' to the festivity itself, frequently one that comprises some form of 'outing'.

Just the cheese

Anything described as being 'just the cheese' could equally be called 'just the thing', for 'cheese' in this sense is borrowed from the Persian and Urdu word *chiz*, meaning 'thing'. Its use in English originated in India where it acquired the familiar spelling, 'cheese'. Once incorporated into the language, the expression became associated with native 'cheeses', giving rise to expressions of enthusiastic approval such as 'That's prime Stilton!'

Keep the pot boiling

For a long time to 'keep the pot boiling' meant earning money to keep the family in food and this sense is maintained in 'pot-boiler', which is often applied to books and other literary works of limited artistic merit that are written primarily to make money. However, 'keeping the pot boiling' also means 'maintaining interest' in a project so that initial enthusiasm does not flag.

Keep your pecker up

When there is a temptation to let your head hang low because you are unhappy or anxious, you may be encouraged to remain cheerful by 'keeping your pecker up'. 'Pecker' here refers to your mouth and by association your face and head in general. 'Keeping your pecker up' means lifting your head and therefore adopting a more confident stance; 'keep your chin up' has the same meaning.

Killing the fatted calf

The parable of the prodigal son as told in St Luke's gospel gave rise to this expression meaning 'to celebrate' and 'to welcome with the best of everything'. In the parable Christ tells the story of two brothers, the elder of whom remains at home, working diligently, while his younger brother takes his share of their inheritance and leaves home to squander it. In time the younger brother sees the error of his ways and returns home in due humility to ask his father for forgiveness and to be allowed back, even in the capacity of a farm labourer. However, his father is so overjoyed to see him again that he offers him presents and arranges a welcoming feast which necessitates 'killing the fatted calf' kept for important celebrations. The elder brother resents the reception his brother has received until his father explains, in the words of the gospel, 'Son, thou art ever with me, and all that I have is thine. It was meet that we should make merry, and be glad: for this thy brother was dead, and is alive again; and was lost, and is found.'

Knowing which side your bread is buttered

Since the sixteenth century 'knowing which side your bread is buttered' has meant knowing and recognizing where your own interests lie.

Knowing your onions

Peeling the closely packed layers of an onion is akin to the intricate study and understanding of a complex issue or problem. By alluding to this, 'knowing your onions' has come to mean that you are 'highly proficient' and 'know your subject inside out'.

Lager beer

In German *Lager* means 'store' and *Lagerbier* is 'beer for storing', in other words beer that should mature in the barrel before being consumed. The English usage of 'lager' and the less common 'lager beer' are direct borrowings from German.

Lamb's wool

Ale is one of the ingredients of 'lamb's wool', an old drink made from the juice of apples roasted in ale, sugar and nutmeg. 'Soft' on the palate, this probably acquired its name from the association with the softness of a 'lamb's wool'.

Land of milk and honey

The Biblical origin of this expression has led to its figurative use in denoting the blessings of heaven. A 'land of milk and honey' is one of great fertility in which nourishing and plentiful food can be produced. The phrase comes from the Book of Exodus, where God tells Moses of the land to which he will lead the children of Israel from captivity in Egypt,

> And I am come down to deliver them out of the hand of the Egyptians, and to bring them up out of that land unto a good land and a large, unto a land flowing with milk and honey.

Larder

The importance of the pig in the diet of our ancestors is revealed in the origin of 'larder', which now refers to a room or cupboard for storing provisions in general. 'Larder' was coined some time before the fourteenth century from the Latin *laridum* (sometimes *lardum*), meaning 'the fat of bacon' and here the close association with the pig becomes evident; for the first 'larders' were principally used to store pig meat in various forms. Only much later were other preserved foods included in the meaning. Until then the pig provided the largest share of preserved and salted meat.

Leg-of-mutton sleeve

A 'leg-of-mutton sleeve' is narrow and close-fitting from wrist to elbow and then balloons out from elbow to shoulder. Its shape is reminiscent of a leg of lamb, or mutton, which gave rise to its name.

Lemon sole

This flatfish owes its name to the French word *limande*, meaning literally a 'flat board'. English usage changed this to 'lemon', thereby losing the visual significance of the French and introducing the citrus fruit with which the origin of the fish has no connection.

Life is just a bowl of cherries

The American musical *Scandals of 1931* included among its songs 'Life is just a bowl of cherries'. Written by Lew Brown, with music by Ray Henderson, this was popularized by Ethel Merman and helped establish the title as a proverbial expression that 'everything is wonderful'.

Limeys

In the eighteenth century British sailors received a free issue of lime juice at sea to protect them from scurvy. This led to the nickname 'limejuicers', abbreviated to 'limeys', by which Britons were known in America and later Australia.

Living high off the hog

The choicest cuts of meat on a pig are found in the upper part of the carcass, and in this expression the reference is to 'eating sumptuously' and therefore 'enjoying considerable affluence', by dining on only the best joints of an animal which at one time was the principal source of meat for most of the population.

Lobster

'Lobster' was the nickname given to British soldiers for several hundred years. The allusion was to a lobster which changed colour and became red when it was cooked, in the same way that a man recruited into the army 'changed colour' when he donned his uniform and became a 'redcoat'. In the seventeenth century certain troops were called 'lobsters' for a different reason. This time it was their 'lobster-tail' helmets which gave rise to the nickname. These were fitted with overlapping plates which protected the back of the wearer's neck.

Lobster Newburg

Delmonico's was *the* fashionable restaurant in late nineteenth-century New York and it was here that 'Lobster Newburg' was first served. The recipe, which appears to have been inspired by a South American dish, requires the lobster to be cooked in a thick, creamy sauce flavoured with brandy, sherry, or wine, with paprika or cayenne pepper and egg yolks. The story runs that it was initially named 'Lobster Wenberg' after Ben Wenberg, a sea-captain and regular patron, who supplied the cayenne pepper and introduced the original South American recipe to Delmonico's. The recipe would still be named after him had he not fallen foul of the proprietors by fighting in their restaurant. They took their revenge and consigned his memory to culinary oblivion by adopting a crude anagram of his name as the new title for the recipe he had inspired; 'Lobster Wenberg' thereafter became 'Lobster Newburg'.

Long spoon to sup with the Devil

This proverb has been recorded since the end of the fourteenth century when Chaucer referred to it in the *Squire's Tale*. The meaning is a warning to 'use caution when dealing with dangerous people'.

Looking for a needle in a bottle of hay

At first glance this expression causes obvious confusion since hay is not a commodity usually associated with the liquids found in 'bottles'. The misunderstanding is natural and arises from an old word spelt the same way as 'bottle', but with an entirely different meaning. 'Bottle', in this alternative sense, was known in English by the fourteenth century and is the anglicized form of the Old French *botel*, which is the diminutive of *botte*, meaning 'a bundle'. So, 'looking for a needle in a bottle of hay', means 'looking for a needle in a bundle of hay' or, to use its now more common version, 'looking for a needle in a haystack'.

Lose in hake, but gain in herring

As hake prey on herring they used to be driven away from herring-fishing grounds. However, fishermen that lost the chance to catch hake, profited from the large stocks of herring which remained. Therefore to 'lose in hake, but gain in herring' is to 'lose one way, but gain in another'.

Loving-Cup

'Loving-cups' form a part of the dining customs in many long-established institutions, such as university colleges and City guilds. The principal of sharing a cup of wine originated in pagan times; the traditional wassail bowl is one such primitive custom that has survived. Monasteries adapted pagan drinking traditions to serve Christianity and introduced the *poculum caritatis*, or 'loving-cup': a large vessel filled with wine which was passed from drinker to drinker, as a mark of unity and fellowship bearing similarities to the Eucharist. Present-day custom often involves the use of a two-handled vessel which is passed around the company at special dinners. Tradition frequently dictates that two people, seated next to each other, stand when the 'loving-cup' reaches them: one to drink from the cup, the other to act as his 'defender'. Once the drinker has taken his or her share, the cup is passed to the 'defender', who drinks, while being 'defended' by the adjacent diner. In this way the 'loving-cup' is passed around, so that all those present are able to share in drinking from the same cup.

Lunch

'Lunch' was probably used in English before its longer form 'luncheon', though both have been recorded since the sixteenth century. To begin with 'lunch' referred to a 'thick piece' or 'hunk' of food and probably originated from the Spanish *longa*, meaning a 'slice'. 'Luncheon' may well have been derived as a simple extension of 'lunch' in the same way that 'truncheon' was an extension of an earlier and shorter word.

Macaroni

Italian wheaten pasta formed into thin tubes gained its name from the Greek word *makaria*, meaning 'barley food'. In the mid-eighteenth century the name was appropriated by a group of dandies who introduced *macaroni* to London dining-tables and styled themselves the Macaroni Club.

Mackerel sky

The pattern of cirrocumulus clouds which have the same rounded shape as the dappled markings of a mackerel's skin is figuratively known as a 'mackerel sky'. The expression is widely used in the forecasting rhyme, 'A mackerel sky won't last twenty-four hours dry'.

Madeleine

Madeleine Paulmier was a nineteenth-century French pastry cook, whose name may well have influenced that of the small fancy sponge cake that is now called a 'madeleine'.

Make mincemeat

'Mincemeat' is an abbreviation of 'minced meat', meat that is cut into very small pieces. Its name is derived from the Latin *minutia*, meaning 'smallness' and 'fineness', via the Old French *mincier*. Used figuratively, 'making mincemeat' of someone means to 'demolish' and 'defeat' them completely.

Marmalade

In Portuguese *marmelada* is 'quince jam' (from *marmelo* the Portuguese for 'quince'). Once oranges became a common fruit in Europe, the English name was transferred to what was effectively 'orange jam'; in Europe *marmelade* still refers to 'jam' in general. It was only right at the end of the eighteenth century that the first modern 'marmalade' was made in Dundee.

Mayonnaise

'Mayonnaise' was originally *mahonnaise*, named after the port of Mahon in Minorca. The island was captured by the French in 1756 and, on going ashore, the commander of the French forces demanded something to eat. With nothing to hand but oil, vinegar, egg yolks and seasoning, his chef beat these together and created the first 'mayonnaise'.

Mealy-mouthed

In German the expression *Mehl im Maule behalten* means 'to carry meal in the mouth', meaning 'lacking straightforwardness in speech'. This may well have influenced the origin of the English 'mealy-mouthed', which means rather 'weak' and 'wishy-washy', 'afraid to call a spade a spade'.

Melba toast

Dame Nellie Melba, the Australian operatic soprano of the late nineteenth and early twentieth centuries, had this type of toast named after her. 'Melba toast', made from very thin slices of bread, was devised in 1897 by the great chef Auguste Escoffier.

Mercury fig

In ancient Rome the first fig gathered from a fig tree was devoted to Mercury. From this a 'Mercury fig' has become a term applied to all first fruits and first works.

Milk run

During the Second World War RAF crews used to refer to regular sorties 'milk runs'. The allusion is to the daily doorstep delivery of milk, which becomes a routine for milkmen who do the same round day after day.

Milky Way

In Greek *gala* means 'milk' and since the fourteenth century 'galaxy', one of the words in English derived from *gala*, has been applied to the group of stars that are known as the Milky Way, which appears to circle the night sky with a milky film of light.

Mint

In Roman mythology Minthe was a nymph beloved of Pluto, god of the underworld. Pluto's wife, Prosperine, who was jealous of Minthe, changed her into a herb that has borne her name ever since. In Latin this became *menta* from which came the French *menthe* and the modern English 'mint'.

Money for jam

Sweet, tasty and comforting, 'jam' has long been given the colloquial meaning of something that is either particularly pleasant, or which is obtained with very little difficulty. Hence the use of 'money for jam' for an unexpected stroke of luck, or a sum of money acquired for little effort.

Mountain dew

In the second half of the eighteenth century small-scale distilling of whisky was banned in Scotland. Demand for whisky remained as strong as ever, however, and illicit stills hidden away in the mountains became the only source of whisky for many Highlanders. They came to refer to it as 'mountain dew', a name which has been applied to illicitly distilled spirits ever since.

Muffin

The soft spongy texture of a 'muffin' may account for the origin of its name. In Old French *pain moufflet* was a type of soft bread, which may have become corrupted in its English version, to produce the soft round 'muffin' which is toasted and eaten with butter.

Mustard gas

Dichlorodiethyl sulphide is a colourless oily liquid with a faint small of garlic and 'mustard'. Released into the atmosphere, it produces a vapour that raises blisters on human skin. During the First World War, it was used against initially unprotected troops, causing blindness and respiratory injuries that made it one of the most feared early examples of modern chemical warfare.

Mutton

'Mutton', like 'beef', reflects the social hierarchy in England following the Norman Conquest. The Old French *moton*, was the precursor to *mouton*, the modern French for 'sheep'. In English it came to mean the 'flesh of the sheep', the meat eaten by the Norman overlords, while their Saxon herdsmen looked after the animals.

Mutton dressed as lamb

This is a derogatory reference to an older woman who dresses to make herself appear younger than she evidently is. In days gone by 'mutton' was slang for a 'prostitute', which may also have had a bearing on the derivation of the expression.

Mutton-chop whiskers

Whiskers that are shaved narrow at the temples and then extend in a triangular shape to the jawline are known as 'mutton-chop whiskers' because their shape resembles that of a mutton chop.

Nappy ale

Not the secret tipple of nanny in the nursery, as the expression might lead one to suppose, 'nappy ale' was used in the eighteenth and nineteenth centuries to describe a strong ale that had a froth, or 'nap', when it was poured.

Nectar

In Greek mythology 'nectar' was the drink of the gods. Along with 'ambrosia', the food which they ate, 'nectar' ensured their immortality. 'Nectar' is a compound of the Greek prefix *nek-* ('death') and the suffix *-tar* (which has the sense of 'triumphing over'). So 'nectar' was a drink which 'triumphed over death' and as such was endowed with a delicious sweet taste. In this way 'nectar' came to refer to any delicious drink and the 'nectarine' was given its name because it was regarded as tasting 'as sweet as nectar'.

Neither barrel the better herring

This is one of several expressions that share a common meaning. 'Much of a muchness' and 'six of one and half-a-dozen of the other' are two of the most common. All imply that two things are so similar that it is virtually impossible to draw a distinction between them. In this case the allusion is to two barrels of herring which are of such similar quality and quantity that there is nothing to choose between them.

Neither fish, flesh, nor fowl

'Fish', 'flesh' and 'fowl' had specific social references in the Middle Ages: fish was the food of the priest, flesh the food of the people in general and fowl all that the poor could afford. Therefore something that was 'neither fish, flesh nor fowl', was not suitable for any class of people and by extension inappropriate in any given circumstances.

Nest egg

The allusion in this expression for 'money laid by' is to the widely used practice of encouraging a hen to lay eggs of her own by placing another egg in her nest. The implication of the expression is that even a small sum of money saved encourages the saver to set more aside, thereby increasing the initial 'deposit' many times over.

Nip

These days the suggestion of a 'nip' of something usually brings to mind a small quantity of whisky. In the eighteenth century, when the word became established in English, it referred to a measure of wine or beer of half-a-pint or less. This was originally called a 'nipperkin', which was related to the Dutch *nippen* of similar meaning.

Not for all the tea in China

From the early part of the twentieth century 'not for all the tea in China' became a popular hyperbole meaning 'under no circumstances', 'not for any consideration'. The expression is believed to have originated in Australia before spreading across the English-speaking world.

Not my cup of tea

This has a similar vintage to 'not for all the tea in China' and, genteel as it appears, has an unequivocal note of censure that something is 'not to my liking'.

Not worth a fig

The 'fig' referred to in this expression is evidently something of very little value, which suggests that it is more likely to be the coarse gesture known as the 'fig of Spain', rather than the tasty fruit of the fig tree. The 'fig of Spain', also known as the 'fico', was well known in Elizabethan England; Shakespeare makes several references to it in his plays. As a gesture of contempt, it was formed by poking the thumb between the first and second fingers. Therefore something that is 'not worth a fig' is not worth anything at all.

Nutty as a fruitcake

The combined association of 'nuts' with being 'daft' and their use in rich fruitcakes gave rise to this turn of phrase, which implies that the person described as 'nutty as a fruitcake' is well and truly 'bonkers'. The 'nut' has been hard done by in the field of mental health. Perhaps its shape and consistency (a hard shell enclosing a softer centre) drew obvious parallels with the head. Hence 'to be off one's nut' or 'to be nuts' meant that you were 'crazy' or 'demented'. By association a lunatic asylum was referred to by the slang 'nuthouse'.

Off his noodle

'Noodle' has been used to describe a 'simpleton' since the middle of the eighteenth century. The derivation of the name is vague, but 'off his noodle' is probably a reference to the older word 'noddle', slang for 'head' from at least the middle of the sixteenth century. In this way anyone who was 'off his noodle' was 'off his head' and therefore crazy.

Old bean

The value of the 'bean', the treasure hunted for in a 'bean feast' in the Middle Ages, may have had something to do with the origin of this good-natured greeting of familiarity, similar in meaning to 'Old chap' and 'Old man'.

Old salt

An 'old salt' is a long-serving sailor; one who has been well 'salted' by his years spent at sea.

On tap

In order to gain access to liquor stored in a cask or barrel, a tap had to be driven into the barrel through which the liquor could be drawn off as needed. At first 'on tap' applied solely to liquor available for immediate consumption; in time, however, the expression was used in a general context to mean anything ready for immediate use.

On the back burner

It was only in the last forty years, after the widespread arrival of electric and gas cookers with multiple hobs that 'on the back burner' became commonly used. Cooks got into the habit of placing pans with slower cooking ingredients on the burners at the back of the cooker, keeping the ones needing greater attention on the burners at the front. Before long 'on the back burner' was being widely used as an indication of something of 'low priority'.

Other fish to fry

Having 'other fish to fry' has been in use in English since the seventeenth century as a way of saying that you have other, better, things to be getting on with. The choice of fish may be connected with the need to eat fish straight from the pan, in order to enjoy it to the full. Therefore 'frying fish' implied setting time aside to prepare it and eat it without interruption.

Out of the frying pan into the fire

Moving 'out of the frying pan into the fire' amounts to moving from one 'hot spot' to another and by implication from one bad situation into one equally as bad. The expression was current in English by the sixteenth century and similar turns of phrase are found in other languages; in ancient Greece, for instance, they talked of getting 'out of the smoke and into the flame'.

Out of the parsley bed

For a couple of hundred years, between the seventeenth and nineteenth centuries, 'out of the parsley bed' was used to describe a 'love child', on the basis that parsley was considered to be an aphrodisiac.

Pea-soup fog

Soup made from dried peas tends to have a dull yellow colour and a thick consistency, both of which applied to the thick fogs and 'smogs' which were a feature of winters in towns and cities in days gone by. The association has persisted and a 'pea-souper' is still a very dense fog.

Peaches and cream complexion

This was the hallmark of feminine beauty at the turn of the twentieth century as advertised and promoted by toiletry and cosmetic manufacturers. The delicate powdery bloom of the peach's skin complemented by a pale creamy colour was regarded as the epitome of healthy living and the 'look' to which all would-be 'beauties' aspired.

Pear-shaped

There are two current uses for 'pear-shaped': one physical, the other metaphorical. The first is an all too apt description of the consequences of middle-aged spread, when the lower portions of the human torso start to be bigger than the upper. This is not infrequently the consequence of becoming a 'couch potato'. In its figurative sense, 'pear-shaped' is applied to situations that have got out of control; the allusion being to a once perfect sphere that has collapsed and consequently sagged with a bulging base.

Pepper and salt

The contrasting colours of pepper (black) and salt (white) have led to their application to circumstances far removed from the kitchen and meal table. One of the commonest is the description of a dark-haired person beginning to go grey, who is frequently described as having 'pepper and salt' on top.

Peppercorn rent

Although a 'peppercorn rent' is deliberately set as a purely nominal payment, it still has all the legal status of a fully contracted rent. 'Peppercorn' rents are levied in the form of a virtual gift, allowing occupation of premises for a very small sum, while allowing the legal owner to retain his or her ultimate rights to the freehold. The term has been used since the Middle Ages when a peppercorn had slightly more value than it does today, but was still recognized as being of no appreciable worth.

Peppery

Anyone described as 'peppery' might also be called 'hot-blooded', 'irascible' or 'easily roused'. Here the sense of 'spirited' is less flattering than in the case of 'pepping up' (described below); far from benefitting from a 'peppery' individual, he or she is best avoided.

Pepping up

'Pep' has been used as an abbreviation for 'pepper' since the middle of the nineteenth century in phrases such as 'full of pep', 'to pep up', 'pep talk' and 'pep pill'. In every case the pungent, stimulating effect of pepper has been applied figuratively in the sense of 'stimulating' and adding 'spirit'.

Pheasant

In the ancient world, Phasis was a river in the land of Colchis, at the eastern edge of the Black Sea in what is present-day Georgia. It was here that Jason and the Argonauts sailed in their quest for the Golden Fleece. According to legend they found birds with long tails and colourful plumage in the land around Phasis and brought some with them when they returned to Greece. The Phasian bird then spread westwards to the rest of Europe. The Romans knew it as *phasianus*. In Old French it was called *faisan*, which became 'pheasant' in English.

Pie-eyed

'Pie-eyed' has been slang for being well and truly drunk since the early years of the twentieth century. Most people in an advanced state of intoxication have difficulty seeing clearly; their eyes are often watery as well. In an effort to focus they tend to open their eyes wider making them rounder than usual. The combined effect of large, watery, blood-shot eyes presumably resembled the appearance of certain types of pie to whoever coined the phrase and before long 'pie-eyed' had been widely adopted as apt description for someone who was suffering from the effects of drinking too much.

Pie in the sky

When this phrase was popularized in the early years of the twentieth century it formed part of a trenchant political and social message. In 1911 a militant Trade Union song book, *Songs of the Workers*, was published and included among its titles

'The Preacher and the Slave' by Joe Hill, which contained the
lines,

> You will eat, bye and bye,
> In that glorious land above the sky;
> Work and pray, live on hay,
> You'll get pie in the sky when you die.

Since then 'pie in the sky' has meant the 'good time' or the 'good
things' that are promised but which never come, or are never
realized.

Piece of cake

The RAF appears to have been responsible for coining this
expression which became widely used in many walks of life by
the end of the Second World War. Its meaning, that something
is 'easy' and 'can be done with little effort', is obscure. The
reference may be that whatever has to be done is as easy 'as
eating cake'. On the other hand, the phrase 'you can't have
your cake and eat it', may have had a part to play in its
evolution. The inference here is that you can't 'have things
both ways' and in either option 'cake' is evidently something to
be desired.

Piecrust table

Tables with intricately carved edges have been called 'piecrust
tables' since the turn of the twentieth century. The reference is
to the decorative finish applied to the edge of piecrusts before
they are baked in the oven.

Playing gooseberry

There seem to be a couple of possible explanations for the origin of this otherwise obscure phrase, applied to a chaperone (or other third party) who makes an awkward threesome while two lovers are romantically occupied. The chaperone was there, of course, for the sake of propriety and may have tactfully spent the time picking gooseberries, to allow the lovers a degree of privacy. On the other hand, anyone 'playing gooseberry' feels foolish and the association with a 'fool' may have led to the punning connection with 'gooseberry fool', the origin of which is described earlier.

Plonk

British troops fighting in France during the First Wold War coined this popular word, which is now generally used to describe most cheap wine. Encountering French white wine, the British soldier soon substituted the word 'plonk' for *vin blanc* ('white wine') and ever since English speakers have been knocking back plonk of every colour from wine-producing countries all over the world.

Ploughman's lunch

A midday meal of bread, cheese and pickle may have been the usual fare for farm workers labouring in the fields for hundreds of years, but the name 'ploughman's lunch' was only coined in the 1970s when the English County Cheese Council hit on it as an advertising slogan. The phrase perfectly captured the spirit of 'old England' fostered by public houses in towns and cities as well as the countryside, and before long the 'ploughman's lunch', later 'ploughman's' on its own, was a permanent feature of the English public house menu.

Pork

In Old English *pigga* or *picga* was the name given to what we call a 'pig'. In ancient Rome, however, a 'pig' was known by the Latin *porcus*, which became *porc* in Old French. Following the Norman Conquest, the distinction between 'pig' and 'pork' became another indication of the social division between Normans and Saxons, similar to that seen with 'beef' and 'mutton'. The Norman word *porc* was used for the flesh of the animal, which the Normans were served at table. Their Saxon servants, on the other hand, retained the name 'pig', since their contact was invariably with the live animal which they tended for their Norman masters.

Pot calling the kettle black

Until cooking stoves and ranges became common kitchen fittings, all cooking vessels had to be heated over open fires. This inevitably led to their being blackened by the flames. This is the allusion in this long-standing expression, which cautions against criticising others for faults you have yourself.

Potatoes and point

At meals where there was nothing to eat but potatoes, children were told to point the potatoes on their plates towards imaginary extras, such as meat, cheese and seasoning, and then eat them. This gave rise to the expression 'potatoes and point' which alludes to a very meagre meal.

Potboiler

The allusion here is to an earlier expression, 'keep the pot boiling'. In this case a 'potboiler' is something which 'keeps the pot boiling', in other words which provides a means of making a living. 'Potboilers' are especially connected with writers who churn out work of questionable artistic merit simply to make money.

Potluck

The pot which was traditionally kept simmering over a kitchen fire is the one referred to here. This was the pot into which any left-overs were put, to bubble away into a thick stew which could be served at mealtimes. Inviting visitors to take 'potluck' implied asking them to join in with eating whatever happened to be in the pot, rather than expecting a specially prepared meal. At table taking 'potluck' amounted to accepting whatever was ladled onto your plate and in its broader meaning the phrase equates to 'taking a chance'.

Pot-pourri

The literal translation of the French *pot-pourri* is 'rotten pot' which scarcely does justice to the delightful fragrance created by the selection of sweet-smelling flower petals and herbs from which 'pot-pourris' are made. 'Pot-pourri' occurs in both French and English in the sense of a musical 'medley' and it still retains an earlier meaning in French as a 'meat-stew'.

Proof of the pudding

In its full wording this old proverb runs 'The proof of the pudding is in the eating' with 'proof' meaning 'test' rather than its normal sense of 'verifying that something is true'. The expression has a long history in English, with the recorded versions dating from the beginning of the fourteenth century. Throughout that time the meaning has remained unaltered. Just as tasting a pudding, rather than looking at it, is the only way to judge how good it is, performance not appearances or promises is the only true test of a person's claims and ability.

Pudding time

In days gone by the first dish set on a meal table was the pudding. Therefore 'pudding time' became equated with 'dinner-time'; the time when food was served and sustenance received. From this 'pudding time' developed its wider meaning of 'the critical time' and 'the nick of time'. So anything happening in 'pudding time' happens at an 'opportune moment'.

Pulling the chestnuts out of the fire

At the heart of this well-known saying is the ancient fable of the monkey and the cat. Seeing chestnuts roasting in the hot embers of a fire, the monkey decides he would like to eat them. However, retrieving the hot chestnuts would mean burning his paws, so he persuades his friend the cat to use his paw to get the chestnuts for him. Since the Middle Ages 'pulling the chestnuts out of the fire' has been used figuratively to meaning 'saving the day', usually for someone else, by retrieving a difficult situation or sparing them embarrassment.

Punch

According to the *Account of East India* written in 1698, the beverage that became popularly known as 'punch' acquired its name from *panch*, the number 'five' in several Indian languages. This referred to the 'five' ingredients from which the drink was traditionally made: spirit, water, spice, sugar and some form of acidic fruit juice. However, by the fifteenth century 'puncheon' was used in English for a large cask, often a container for wine; so the origin of 'punch' may lie in an abbreviation of 'puncheon'. There is no question, though, that 'punch' spread to other European languages from English and since this occurred as trade with India was developing, the Indian associations of 'punch' must have had some influence on its development.

Putting new wine into old bottles

The allusion in this proverb is to the warning given by Christ in St Matthew's gospel, 'Neither do men put new wine into old bottle: else the bottles break, and the wine runneth out, and the bottles perish: but they that put new wine into new bottles, and both are preserved'. The bottles referred to were animal skins which, if old, were liable to split as new wine fermented inside them; new skins, however, were still sufficiently flexible to expand with the fermentation. In its figurative sense the proverb means that new ideas and practices cannot be successfully imposed on people who are too set in their old ways to cope with the pressure of adjusting to them.

Putting salt on his tail

This used to be the advice given to children who wanted to catch a bird; if they laid salt on its tail, they would stand a much better chance of catching it. In the same sense 'putting salt on his tail' was transferred to people with the meaning of 'catching' or 'apprehending' someone.

Putting the miller's eye out

The meaning of 'putting the miller's eye out' is similar to that of 'drowning the miller', referred to earlier. Here criticism is focused on a pudding, or broth, that has been made so thin that even the keen eye of a miller would be hard put to spot any flour in it.

Quarrel with your bread and butter

Since 'bread and butter' is applied to the fundamentals of life, such as basic food and the means of making a living, 'quarrelling with your bread and butter' means acting against your own interests, specifically with regard to recklessly giving up your job, or doing anything else that will deprive you of your living.

Ragout

Stews made by combining meat and vegetables have been known as 'ragouts' in English since the seventeenth century. 'Ragout', like many cookery expressions, is French in origin, coming from *ragoûter*, derived from the Latin *regustare* ('to taste again'). Both the Latin and French words have the sense of 'restoring taste', which in the case of a 'ragout' probably refers to the spicy seasoning added to it.

Red herring

Understanding how 'red herring' came by its current usage is complicated by the fact that only part of the original saying is used today. The complete expression is 'drawing a red herring across the path' in which the 'herring' was dried, smoked and salted in much the same way as a kipper. Like a kipper, a 'red herring' had a strong smell and it was popularly believed that if a 'red herring' was drawn across the path taken by a fox, it would cover its scent and divert pursuing hounds into following a false trail. In its present-day, abbreviated, form a 'red herring' represents anything that is used to divert attention from the principal issue that is being investigated or considered.

Rehash

As discussed earlier, 'hash' is a meal made from chopped-up leftovers; scraps of food that have already been served once and are now being recycled. In the case of 'rehash' the allusion is more favourable than the derogatory connotations of expressions like 'making a hash of'. To 'rehash' something, is to reconsider it, metaphorically to cut it up even finer than before and examine all the ins and outs, before reaching a final conclusion.

Riddle of claret

'A riddle of claret' is a specific quantity of claret: thirteen bottles, comprising a magnum and twelve quarts. This was the amount customarily presented to some golf clubs by magistrates invited to celebration dinners. In accordance with tradition, the gift of claret was sent in a 'riddle', or coarse-meshed sieve.

Rod in pickle

Having 'a rod in pickle' means to 'have an unpleasant surprise in store for someone'. The allusion is to corporal punishment, which was once a regular feature of education and chastisement in general. Birch rods used to administer such a beating were kept in brine (pickle) to ensure that the twigs remained supple.

Rotten apple

For as long as apples have been harvested and stored, wise apple-growers have avoided letting them touch each other in the knowledge that a rotten apple will spread its disease by contact. There are many proverbs based on this, such as: 'a rotten apple quickly infects its neighbour', which is the translation of an old Latin proverb; 'the rotten apple injures its neighbour' and 'the rotten apple spoils its companion'. In its figurative sense a 'rotten apple' refers to someone whose presence and influence has a demoralizing or otherwise deleterious effect on others, especially those in close proximity.

Row of beans

As one of the most readily available vegetables, the bean has frequently been regarded with low esteem. This phrase is usually used in a negative context such as, 'He isn't worth a row of beans', or 'I wouldn't give a row of beans for that', which values the bean as being of very little worth, even when it is sown in the traditional way to produce part of a crop.

Rub salt in the wound

Salt added to open wounds makes them sting and hurt even more. Therefore deliberately 'rubbing salt in the wound' is an action calculated to increase pain and discomfort. In its figurative use the phrase is applied to making an already painful subject worse. The same sense may be applied to 'rubbing something in', whereby an unpleasant situation is emphasized in order to prove a point, set an example, or exact revenge.

Salad days

William Shakespeare is credited with coining this phrase, which he gave to Cleopatra in lines spoken by her right at the end of Act One of *Antony and Cleopatra*,

> My salad days
> When I was green in judgement, cold in blood
> To say as I said then.

The 'salad days' referred to by the Queen of Egypt was the period earlier in her life when she had an affair with Julius Caesar, before she and Mark Antony fell in love. From Shakespeare, the phrase has become widely used to describe days of youth and inexperience. Julian Slade borrowed it for his popular 1954 musical, *Salad Days*.

Salt away

Before refrigeration was widely available, preserving food in brine or barrels of salt was a common method of setting aside provisions for future consumption. Whether as a supply of food during the unproductive months of winter, or on a sea voyage when fresh food was unavailable, salted food could be a life-saver on occasions. The value attached to it gave rise to the expression to 'salt away', which has the sense of 'storing' or 'preserving for future use'; it is applied in particular to money that is 'salted away' as a safeguard against lean times in the future.

Salt of the earth

The best people in every sense have been called the 'salt of the earth' since Christ used the phrase in the Sermon on the Mount, as related in St Matthew's gospel. After describing the beatitudes of the 'blessed', Christ told his disciples, 'Rejoice, and be exceeding glad: for great is your reward in heaven: for so persecuted they the prophets which were before you. Ye are the salt of the earth'.

Sandwich

The idea of placing food between two slices of bread may not have been dreamed up by John Montagu, 4th Earl of Sandwich, but it was he who popularized it and gave the 'sandwich' its name. His lordship was an inveterate gambler, who would sit at the gaming-table for hours on end (once for twenty-four hours non-stop). Such was his passion for cards that he begrudged having to leave them for meals, so he got into the habit of calling for slices of meat between two pieces of bread which he could eat without the need to stop his card-play. For a time the Earl of Sandwich served as First Lord of the Admiralty and Captain Cook named the Sandwich Islands, in what is now Hawaii, after him.

Sandwich-man

Men who carry advertising boards front and back as they walk about the streets have been known as 'sandwich-men' since the middle of the nineteenth century. The allusion to the 'sandwich' comes from the method of carrying the boards, which are supported on straps slung over the carrier's shoulders, giving him the appearance of being 'sandwiched' between the two boards.

Sardine

The island of Sardinia and the small member of the herring family, called the 'sardine' in English, are closely related in their Greek and Latin names; one no doubt giving its name to the other, though which came first is uncertain. Sardines are caught all over the Mediterranean, not just in the waters around Sardinia.

Sauce

Liquid preparations of many flavours that are added to all sorts of food have been known as 'sauces' in English since the fourteenth century. The English usage is a direct borrowing from French, which in turn came from the Latin *salsus*. However, *salsus* means 'flavoured with salt' and it took hundreds of years for the term to be applied to the range of sauces prepared by cooks today. In Roman times 'sauces' were effectively side-dishes of vegetables seasoned with salt which accompanied the main course. No doubt the idea of adding 'seasoning' to enhance the flavour of food lay at the root of the usage of 'sauce' to mean 'insolence' and 'impertinence', in phrases like 'saucy devil!' and the ironic 'I like your sauce!'

Saving your bacon

The act of 'saving your bacon' is more than preventing an accidental spillage from your plate. As the only meat available to a large proportion of the population for hundreds of years, 'bacon' was a vital commodity. Cured and dried, 'bacon' was preserved to supply essential food during the winter, and 'saving your bacon' from any form of loss or damage amounted almost to a life-saving act. Therefore, in 'saving your bacon' you are saving yourself from injury, loss or other disaster.

Say 'Cheese'

Since the 1920s it has been common for photographers to get their subjects to smile by asking them to say 'cheese'. A look in the mirror will confirm that 'saying "cheese"' does put the lips in a position similar to a smile.

Saying grace

'Grace' said before a meal asks for blessing on food about to be eaten; 'grace' said after a meal, gives thanks for that food. Until the fourteenth century the phrase was commonly used in the plural ('graces'), following the French for 'thanks', *grâces*. In its earliest English usage it formed part of the old phrase to 'do graces' or to 'give graces', which again followed the French phrase of the same meaning, *rendre grâces*.

Selling like hot cakes

In America 'pancakes' have been called 'hot cakes' for over three hundred years. As a popular feature of the American diet, 'hot cakes' are cooked and sold at many social gatherings and such is the demand for them that they are often sold as soon as they are cooked. So anything which 'sells likes hot cakes' sells immediately it goes on sale, resulting in a commercial triumph.

Serving the same sauce

This expression means to 'give as good as you get' and to 'retaliate' in kind. Here sauce is seen as a common denominator, in this instance in an argument or conflict, much as it is in the expression 'what's sauce for the goose is sauce for the gander'.

Settling on the lees

In wine making, the lees are the dregs and sediment left at the bottom of a bottle or barrel: a waste product that no one wants. 'Settling on the lees' develops this sense of 'left-overs' and 'waste' in its meaning of 'settling down to live on what is left' after squandering most of your fortune. In a similar way it implies 'making the best of a bad job'.

Shoeing the goose

The idea of 'shoeing a goose' in the same way that one 'shoes' a horse is, of course, farcical. And that is the purpose of this expression. In its use of hyperbole, it points up the absurdity of the idea and by association implies how time can be wasted on unnecessary work and, worse still, how it can be frittered away by spending time on trifles rather than concentrating on things which really need to be done.

Short commons

At one time students at the universities of Oxford and Cambridge were served all their meals at common tables in their college halls. 'Commons' was the name given to the food served at breakfast and anyone receiving 'short commons' got 'short rations', in other words he was given only a 'scanty meal'.

Silver spoon in your mouth

Silver spoons used to be common christening presents, however this phrase alludes to the children of well-to-do parents. They had no need to wait until their christenings before getting their silver spoons. They would have silver spoons (and all the wealth that their use implied) from the moment they were born.

Sirloin

There have been various stories told of at least three English kings who were said to have 'knighted' this particular joint of beef, thereby accounting for the 'sir' in 'sirloin'. However, the history of the word shows that what is now spelt 'sirloin' should really be spelt 'surloin'. This is because the word originated in Old French as *surloigne*, meaning 'above the loin', with reference to the position of the 'sirloin' joint immediately above the 'loin'. To add to the confusion, a 'baron' of beef, which is two unseparated 'sirloins', acquired its name through the inaccurate spelling of 'sur/sir'; the assumption being that a 'baron' was ranked higher than a knight.

Slippery as an eel

Eels crop up in several expressions and all draw on the difficulty of grasping an eel and preventing it from slipping away. 'Holding the eel of science by the tail' means to have a smattering of a subject, which is likely to slip from the memory as easily as an eel would slip from your grasp if held by the tail. Therefore anyone described as being as 'slippery as an eel' is regarded as being very evasive and, in certain cases, dishonest.

Small beer

'Small' in this expression means 'weak', because 'small beer' was beer brewed with a low level of alcohol. Unlike stronger, more alcoholic beers, 'small beer' did not 'pack a punch', nor did it need to be 'treated with respect' to avoid becoming intoxicated by it. By analogy, 'trivialities' and people regarded as being of 'little consequence' were dismissed as being 'small beer'.

Smart cookie

In Scotland a 'cookie' is a 'bun', whereas in America it is a biscuit, probably from the Dutch *koekje*, which is the diminutive of *koek* ('cake'). In America 'cookie' became a term of endearment during the twentieth century and the term 'smart cookie' was bestowed on those blessed with shrewdness and quick wits.

Sour grapes

The disparaging tone of 'sour grapes' touches on a deeply-rooted failing in human nature. This was taken up by Aesop in his fable about the fox who spotted a bunch of grapes and tried in vain to eat them. Only when he realized that they were beyond his reach did he lose his initial enthusiasm. Turning away from the grapes, he dismissed the idea of eating them claiming that they were sour anyway. The story and its theme gained currency and, in time, something disparaged because it is beyond one's reach, was referred to as 'sour grapes'.

Spare at the spigot and spill at the bung

A 'spigot' is a small peg which is inserted into the vent hole of a barrel or cask and here the allusion is to one filled with beer or wine. In this instance the owner displays his meanness over small things by taking care not to waste any of the barrel's contents at the vent hole, while overlooking the main bung sealing the barrel, through which his drink is leaking in profusion. So, to 'spare at the spigot and spill at the bung' is to be tight-fisted about things which don't really matter, while being wasteful when it comes to those which really are important.

Spilling the beans

'Spilling the beans' is the inadvertent divulging of information which would otherwise have been kept secret. One explanation places the origin of the phrase in ancient Greece, where it was customary for beans of two different colours to be used in secret ballots, held among members of an organization to which a would-be member was applying. Those in favour of his joining voted with a white bean, signifying 'yes'; a brown bean counted as a 'no' vote. When all votes had been cast, the beans were counted in secret, so that the prospective member would have no idea how many votes there were for and against him. The only way he could discover this was if the beans were accidentally spilt in his presence. Another line of thought follows the idea that some fortune tellers, instead of using crystal balls or tea leaves, rely on spilling beans from a cup and then interpreting the future from the pattern made by them.

Spoon-fed

From the turn of the twentieth century 'spoon-fed' has been used to describe two types of people who are prevented from acting independently. One group are those who are so cosseted and pampered that they are treated like babies. The others suffer a form of brainwashing and are prevented from thinking for themselves by being 'spoon fed' ideas and information that they consume without questioning.

Spring chicken

This American expression is usually used in the negative, when a man or woman described as 'no spring chicken' is unkindly referred to as being 'no longer young.' 'Chicken' and 'chick' were slang expressions for girls and young women from the eighteenth century. 'Spring chickens' came into use at the beginning of the twentieth century, although its use is nonsensical when women are referred to, because in the poultry business 'spring chicken' are young cockerels sent to market in the autumn.

Square meal

A 'square meal' is one that satisfies the eater. 'Square' in this context means 'complete' and 'full', just as a 'square' figure encompasses its area in four clearly delineated lines.

Staff of life

Since Biblical times 'bread' has been regarded as one of mankind's basic foods, something simple and nourishing on which he could rely when other, more exotic, food was wanting. As such, bread was regarded as an important element in human existence and from early Egyptian times it was described as being 'the staff of life', the prop and support on which human existence could depend.

Stew in your own juice

Those who 'stew in their own juice' suffer the consequences of their actions and, by implication, suffer them for a considerable length of time. 'Stewing', both culinary and metaphorical, involves a slow, simmering process. Inside an enclosed cooking vessel, a mixture of meat and vegetables is gently 'stewed' to produce a succulent, tasty meal in which the liquor the food has been cooking in is as important a factor in its taste as the solid ingredients.

Storm in a teacup

Here is another use of hyperbole to point up the absurdity of a situation. At the risk of stating the obvious, a genteel cup of tea is not the place in which to find a 'storm'. However, the very circumstances in which tea is drunk from teacups, imply that even slight deviations from the accepted code of conduct and conversation can cause ructions completely out of proportion to the real nature of any 'offence'. A 'storm in a teacup', therefore, is a 'great fuss made about something of no consequence'.

Strawberry blonde

Blonde hair with an attractive reddish tint is known as 'strawberry blonde' and a woman with hair that colour can herself be described as a 'strawberry blonde' by those who classify people by the colour of their hair.

Sundae

At one time there was a law in the State of Virginia which prohibited the sale of soda-fountain drinks on Sundays. However, demand for such drinks on Sundays was such that an enterprising owner of a drugstore in Norfolk, Virginia, created a 'thickened' drink by adding fruit and ice-cream to his soda-fountain drinks. Once the consistency of the drink reached a legally defined level it became classified as a meal, as far as the law was concerned, and was no longer restricted to Monday-Saturday sales. From the point of view of the drugstore customers it was a 'Sunday' drink and before long had acquired the name 'sundae'.

Taking the biscuit

To 'take the biscuit' can be interpreted in two ways, depending whether it is being used ironically or not. As a straightforward statement of approbation, 'taking the biscuit' means being 'the best of the lot', even 'being incredible'. However, it is commonly used to express a strong degree of irony, in expressions like 'I've heard some daft things in my time, but that takes the biscuit!' 'Taking the biscuit' is an anglicized form of an expression common in America from the middle of the nineteenth century. The American expression refers to 'taking the cake', an allusion to the cake awarded to the winners of a 'cakewalk'. This was a nineteenth-century pastime, popular with Black Americans, in which couples walked arm in arm around a room. The couple judged to be the most graceful walkers 'took the cake' as their prize.

Taking the say

'Taking the say' is an abbreviated form of 'taking the assay'. These days an 'assay' is a test applied to metal alloys, but in the sixteenth century it was applied to 'tests' in general; in the case of 'taking the say', the 'test' was one on food and drink. In an age when assassination by poisoning was not unknown, food and drink prepared for anyone liable to be assassinated was 'tested' and 'tasted' before it was laid before them, in order to prove that it was safe to be consumed.

Talking turkey

This expression originated in America where it was in common usage by the middle of the nineteenth century, before spreading throughout the English-speaking world. 'Talking turkey' means 'talking business', or 'talking seriously'. It appears to date from the early days of the colonies, when turkeys formed an important part of the trade between the Indians and the Pilgrim Fathers. Before long the Indians realized that every trading visit would involve their supplying turkeys and 'You come to talk turkey?' became a familiar saying whenever a colonist appeared to discuss business.

Tea and sympathy

'Tea and sympathy' has come to refer to a sympathetic listener who offers comfort to someone in distress. It was known by the twentieth century, but gained a boost when it was used as the title for a 1956 film starring Deborah Kerr. This was based on a play of the same name by Robert Anderson which told the story of a schoolboy's affair with a teacher's wife.

Teetotal

Anyone claiming to be 'teetotal' abstains from all types of alcoholic drink and such abstainers have been described as 'teetotal' since the middle of the nineteenth century. 'Teetotal' came into use on both sides of the Atlantic at more or less the same time, though each has a distinct origin of its own. In England the word appears to have been coined by Dick Turner of Preston in Lancashire. Speaking at a meeting in September 1833, he declared the need for complete abstinence and emphasized the point by telling his audience that 'nothing but the te-te-total will do.' Such was the success of his speech, that 'teetotal' was quickly adopted as the name for total abstinence and his tombstone bears the inscription,

> Beneath this stone are deposited the remains of Richard Turner, author of the word *Teetotal* as applied to abstinence from all intoxicating liquors, who departed this life on the 27th day of October, 1846, aged 56 years.

In America 'teetotal' may have appeared slightly earlier as a result of campaigning by the New York Temperance Society. Members who signed the 'pledge' had 'O.P.' (standing for Old Pledge) entered against their names if they undertook to abstain from distilled spirits only. Those who pledged to abstain from all forms of alcohol had a 'T' for 'total abstinence' entered against their names. The regular use of 'T-total' soon led to the spelling 'teetotal'.

That's the way the cookie crumbles

The American 'cookie' takes its name from the Dutch *koekje* meaning a 'little cake'; in Britain 'cookie' equates with 'biscuit'. 'That's the way the cookie crumbles' gained in popularity after the Second World War as a fatalistic expression meaning 'what will be, will be', usually when something turns out less promisingly than expected. It was popularized by American advertisements of the 1950s but is now widely used in the English-speaking world as a whole.

The answer is a lemon

This is a form of response meaning 'nothing doing', which is given in reply to a request or question that the speaker regards as being unreasonable or ridiculous. The tart taste of lemon juice has caused the fruit to be associated with the negative side of many issues and in this case 'the answer is a lemon' amounts to saying 'you must be joking!'

The fat is in the fire

Anyone who has cooked over an open fire knows the hazards of letting grease or fat fall into the flames. The fire flares up, black smoke billows forth and there is a good chance that the food being cooked may be spoiled. Since most cooking took place over open fires until as recently as the nineteenth century, fat falling into the fire was a constant problem and worry. The expression occurs in various forms in several languages and 'the fat is in the fire' has been used in English since the Middle Ages in the sense of something having been let out accidentally which results in a 'flare-up'.

The mill cannot grind with the water that is past

This old proverb dates from a time when watermills ground much of the flour in England; it was first recorded in the early years of the seventeenth century. The implication of 'the mill cannot grind with the water that is past' is that you need to take opportunities when they are presented, because once they have moved past you they cannot be retrieved.

The moon is made of green cheese

Anyone who believes that 'the moon is made of green cheese' must be a simpleton; that, at least, is the gist of this long-established expression, known in English for nearly five hundred years. In all that time the meaning has not changed. 'The moon is made of green cheese' still means what it did when Henry VIII was King of England, in the sense of a statement of absolute credulity. Anyone who believes something as absurd as that would believe anything.

There's no such thing as a free lunch

The idea that you cannot get something for nothing had been in circulation long before the phrase 'there's no such thing as a free lunch' was coined in America during the nineteenth century. The expression, which was enthusiastically adopted by economists in the second half of the twentieth century, appears to have developed from the practice of some saloons which offered 'free' food to those who patronized them in order to drink. One imagines that the prices of drinks were raised accordingly, because many saloons exhibited signs warning 'No free lunch here' to anyone hoping to eat without buying a drink. The practice had died out before the First World War, partly because of changes to licensing and health legislation that tightened up on the insanitary conditions in which 'free lunches' were served in the less salubrious establishments.

The world's mine oyster

Oysters were recognized as both a source of nourishment and as the producers of pearls in the Middle Ages. Shakespeare made use of 'the world's mine oyster' in the sense of 'the world is the place from which a profit can be extracted', when he gave Pistol the line after Falstaff has refused to lend him a penny in the second act of *The Merry Wives of Windsor*,

Why, then the world's mine oyster,
Which I with sword will open.

Thinking small potatoes

The potato arrived in English-speaking countries less than five hundred years ago, in spite of which it soon became well embedded in several common expressions, of which 'thinking small potatoes' is one of the oldest. 'Small potatoes' means 'something of little consequence', and 'thinking small potatoes' is 'regarding something as being of very little importance'. At the end of the eighteenth century, British usage referred to 'little potatoes', but 'small potatoes' became the standard phrase in America and has now been adopted in other English-speaking countries.

Titbit

A tasty morsel, known as a 'titbit' since the seventeenth century, was first coined as 'tydbit' or 'tidbit'. This was a combination of 'tid' meaning 'nice' and 'soft', with 'bit' derived from 'bite'. Placed together, 'tidbit/titbit' carried the sense of something which had been 'bitten off'.

To go the whole hog

'To go the whole hog' means to do something 'completely and thoroughly', with 'no half measures'. The expression may have derived from the practice of using every part of the household pig, leaving nothing to waste after the animal had been butchered to set meat aside for the winter. Another explanation rests on a different meaning of 'hog', which, from the end of the seventeenth century was slang for a 'shilling'. In this context 'to go the whole hog' means 'to spend the whole shilling at once.' In both cases the phrase has an air of determination and resolution that survives today.

To have a bone to pick

'To have a bone to pick' with someone means that you have something disagreeable to discuss and settle with them. The allusion is to a bone thrown to dogs, which inevitably leads to snarling and fighting as each tries to win the bone for its own enjoyment.

To have your cake and eat it

John Heywood recorded this proverb in his *Dialogue of Proverbs* in 1546. The version he noted was, 'I trowe ye raue, Wolde ye bothe eate your cake, and have your cake?' The wording may have changed since then ('eat' and 'have' are interchangeable in all versions) but the meaning has remained the same: 'you cannot have it both ways'. Once the cake has been 'eaten', it cannot be retained in your possession. When the reference is to money, the implication is that money spent cannot be spent a second time; nor can it be saved.

To cry cockles

This grim expression came into being when executions were still held in public. From the late eighteenth century to the middle of the nineteenth 'To cry cockles' was slang for 'to be hanged'. The association comes from the gurgling sound of strangulation.

Toffee-nosed

Describing someone as 'toffee-nosed' implies that they are 'stuck-up', giving themselves pretensions with the aim of appearing superior. While it is tempting to link the stickiness of 'toffee' with the allusion to being 'stuck up', the latter refers to the male peacock, whose magnificent tail plumage is 'stuck up' as a sign of his superiority over others. 'Toffee-nosed' may owe more to the nineteenth-century slang 'toff'. This was a term applied to noblemen and gentlemen commoners: students of aristocratic backgrounds at the university of Oxford who were allowed to wear caps ('mortar boards') with gold tassels, or tufts. 'Toff' is a corruption of 'tuft', so someone who sets themselves up as a 'toff' and adopts a haughty demeanour could well be described as 'toffee-nosed'.

Too many cooks spoil the broth

As one of the best known 'food' proverbs, 'too many cooks spoil the broth' has been recorded in English since Shakespeare's time. Its meaning, which has remained unaltered, is that if too many people take part in an undertaking its chances of success will be prejudiced.

Tough cookie

In the expression 'smart cookie', 'cookie' is an endearment used in much the same way as 'sweetheart'. However, such an endearment would be inappropriate in the case of 'tough cookie', which describes an intractable person, best summed up as an 'awkward customer'.

Tripe

'Tripe' was once a more popular dish than it is today. Formed from the first or second stomach of an ox, tripe was eaten in ancient times and was widely enjoyed throughout Europe. By the nineteenth century, however, 'tripe' or a 'bag of tripe' was a term of a disparagement in English slang. By the beginning of the twentieth century 'tripe' was starting to be seen as an inferior type of food and so became associated with 'rubbish' and 'complete nonsense'. This applied particularly when 'tripe' referred to writing, acting or singing of a very inferior standard and this is the sense in which it is used today.

True blue will never stain

A 'true blue' is a person who is constant, loyal, faithful and reliable. Such a person is reckoned never to disgrace himself and the allusion in 'true blue will never stain' is to the blue aprons traditionally worn by butchers, which do not show blood stains.

True to your salt

'Salt' in this context means 'salary', which comes from the Latin *salarius* meaning 'to do with salt' and refers to the allowance paid to Roman soldiers to buy salt. Therefore, anyone said to be 'true to his salt', was 'true to his salary' and by association 'true to his employers'.

Up corn, down horn

This old saying refers to variations of commodity prices in the agricultural market. 'Corn' applies to cereal crops; 'horn' to beef. 'Up corn, down horn' means that when the price of corn is high (making it expensive), the price of beef is low (making it cheap), because people have less money to spend on meat.

Upper crust

One explanation for the origin of this phrase lies in what was believed to be a time-honoured practice of offering the upper crust of a loaf of bread to the most honoured guest seated at table. This was regarded as the tastiest part of the loaf and therefore gave that particular guest the best share. Another suggestion is that the 'upper crust' referred to is in fact a pie crust, which is reckoned to be the best part of a pie. In both explanations 'upper crust' has a sense of superiority and this is the meaning to which it is put figuratively in referring to an 'élite', or 'highest social class'.

Venison

'Venison' has a very specific meaning today as the flesh of a deer, but this is comparatively recent. When 'venison' was first recorded in English in the thirteenth century, it referred to the flesh of any animal killed in a hunt. The original meaning and the word itself originated from the Latin *venatio*, the noun for 'hunting' or 'the chase'.

Vintage

'Vintage' is the English form of the French *vendange*, the 'wine harvest' that takes place each autumn when the grapes are picked. That is why 'vintage' is the word used to classify wines by year. Wines of a good 'vintage' were made in a year when the growing conditions resulted in a harvest of grapes of very high quality. Therefore wine from a good *vendange* is known in English as 'vintage wine'; and from this 'vintage year' has been applied to memorable or noteworthy years in any context. 'Vintage' and *vendange* originated from the Latin for 'a grape-gathering, *vindemenia*, which is a compound of *vinum* ('wine' or 'grapes') and the verb *demere* ('to take away').

Vol-au-vent

The literal translation from French for this popular pastry case filled with creamed meat or chicken is 'flight on the wind'. This probably alludes to the very light puff-pastry from which the case of a vol-au-vent is made.

Waffle

'Waffle' is a word originally coined in America from the Dutch *wafel*, both of which are used for a batter-cake baked in a gridlike pattern between two irons of that shape. Since the end of the nineteenth century 'waffle' has acquired the pejorative meaning of 'nonsense' and 'meaningless chatter'. This may be due to its similarity to a number of similar words. Two of the strongest contenders are a Scottish word, 'waffle, meaning to 'flutter' or 'flap', and the dialect use of 'waffle' for the yelping sound made by a small dog.

Walking on eggshells

Treading very lightly, in the metaphorical sense of trying not to cause any disturbance, has used the analogy of walking on 'eggshells' (sometimes 'eggs') since the seventeenth century.

Waygoose

By tradition a goose was served at the annual entertainment given to printers, which was originally held at Bartholomew-tide (24 August), when working by candle-light began. The term was later applied to an annual feast held in the summer. The origin of 'wayzgoose' appears to be from 'wayz' an obsolete word for 'stubble', which may have referred to a goose allowed to feed on the corn dropped among the stubble during harvest, which would have started a few weeks before Bartholomew-tide.

Welsh rarebit

When 'Welsh rarebit' was first coined, it was known as 'Welsh rabbit'. This was the name by which the dish of melted cheese and seasoning, poured over buttered toast, was known until the end of the eighteenth century, when 'rabbit' was changed to 'rarebit'. The reason for this appears to have been lexical interference by a dictionary compiler. Unable to find any connection between the dish and a rabbit, he seems to have decided to change the name to something more appropriate. The name 'Welsh rarebit' has stuck, but had 'Welsh rabbit' been allowed to survive it would have sat happily in the dictionary alongside other culinary anomalies like 'Bombay duck', which is really a fish, and 'mock turtle soup' which is made from a calf's head.

Wetting your whistle

'Wetting your whistle' as an idiom was in common use when Chaucer was writing the *Canterbury Tales* at the end of the fourteenth century; he uses it in the 'Reeve's Tale', in the line 'So was hir joly whistle wel ywet'. The meaning is the same now as it was then: 'wetting your whistle' equates to 'having a drink.'

What's sauce for the goose is sauce for the gander

This is a proverb dating from the seventeenth century which means 'what is suitable for a woman is suitable for a man'. An earlier version makes the same assertion with cattle, but this has not stood the test of time. The wording of the proverb appears in different forms as well, but the meaning has remained the same throughout its history.

Where's the beef?

'Where's the beef?' became a watchword in the 1984 US presidential election campaign. Walter Mondale, who was canvassing for, and eventually won, the Democratic Party nomination, used 'Where's the beef?' to great effect in pointing up the inadequacies of his rivals' arguments and promises. The phrase had actually been coined as part of a nationwide advertising campaign by the Wendy's hamburger chain. This included a television commercial featuring three elderly ladies who ordered hamburgers in a restaurant styled 'home of the Big Bun'. While there was no disputing the size of the bun, the tiny sliver of meat inside was not to their liking and one of the trio was moved to telephone the restaurant manager to demand angrily, 'Where's the beef?' From this, the phrase acquired its broader meaning of questioning the substance of a statement or promise made by someone else.

Whisky

'Whisky' is the modern name for the famous spirit distilled (with this spelling) in Scotland from malted barley; in Ireland and America the spirit is known as 'whiskey'. It comes from the Gaelic *uisgebeatha*, meaning 'the water of life' in the same sense as *aqua vita* in Latin and *eau de vie* in French.

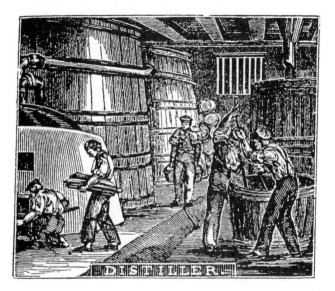

With a pinch of salt

Anything taken 'with a pinch of salt' is treated with the utmost suspicion. Just as a 'pinch of salt' may help you swallow otherwise unpalatable food, so a metaphoric 'pinch of salt' enables you to accept something dubious by granting it a mere grain of truth.

Without a bean

The fact that beans are so common and once formed an important part of the poor man's diet means that they have been regarded as having little financial value. The story of Jack and the Beanstalk confirms this: Jack's mother is furious when he comes home having 'sold' their cow for a handful of beans. So to be 'without a bean' is to be very hard up, as in the expression 'I haven't a bean' which means 'I haven't any money at all'.

Working for peanuts

'Peanuts' are not really nuts. Strictly speaking they are legumes and belong to the same family as peas. In fact 'peanuts' are about the same size as peas, which makes them smaller than most other nuts and it is their size which has led to their being associated with 'meagreness'. This applies particularly when peanuts are used metaphorically for money and therefore anyone 'working for peanuts' is working for something very small, in other words for 'very low wages'.

Worth his salt

This is another instance in which salt is used in the sense of 'salary', from the Latin *salarium*, the salt allowance paid to Roman soldiers. Anyone 'worth his salt' was acknowledged to be a good worker who justified the wages paid to him. The expression is more often used in the negative, in the sense of an idle or inefficient worker who is certainly 'not worth his salt'.

You can't make a soufflé rise twice

A 'soufflé' is a light fluffy baked egg dish, made by mixing a thick sauce or purée with the yolks and stiffly beaten whites of eggs. The secret of its success is serving it directly from the oven, before it begins to sag and lose its consistency. The one thing the great majority of cooks are unable to do is to 'make a soufflé rise twice'. The expression gained wider currency in the twentieth century in the sense of 'it is pointless trying make something happen a second time if it is unrepeatable'. The wider implication of the expression is that a unique event should be allowed to remain unique, since trying to recreate it will only debase the memory of the original.

You can't make an omelette without breaking eggs

'You can't make an omelette without breaking eggs' is a direct translation of a French proverb. It carries a warning to anyone who hopes to 'get something for nothing' that unless they are prepared to make the necessary effort or sacrifice to achieve their objective, they are unlikely to succeed.